D0910329

WITHDRAWN

Never-Ending Nightmare

Never-Ending Nightmare

The Neoliberal Assault on Democracy

Pierre Dardot and
Christian Laval

Translated by
Gregory Elliott

VERSO
London • New York

Avec le soutien du

This work was published with the help of the French
Ministry of Culture – Centre national du livre
Ouvrage publié avec le concours du Ministère français
chargé de la culture – Centre national du livre

Cet ouvrage publié dans le cadre du programme d'aide à la publication bénéficie
du soutien du Ministère des Affaires Etrangères et du Service Culturel de
l'Ambassade de France représenté aux Etats-Unis. This work received support
from the French Ministry of Foreign Affairs and the Cultural Services of the French
Embassy in the United States through their publishing assistance program.

First published in English by Verso 2019
First published as *Ce cauchemar qui n'en finit pas: Comment le
néolibéralisme défait la démocratie* © Editions La Découverte 2016
Translation © Gregory Elliott 2019

1 3 5 7 9 10 8 6 4 2

Verso
UK: 6 Meard Street, London W1F 0EG
US: 20 Jay Street, Suite 1010, Brooklyn, NY 11201
versobooks.com

Verso is the imprint of New Left Books

ISBN-13: 978-1-78663-474-0 (HB)
ISBN-13: 978-1-78663-476-4 (US EBK)
ISBN-13: 978-1-78663-475-7 (UK EBK)

British Library Cataloguing in Publication Data
A catalogue record for this book is available from the British Library

Library of Congress Cataloging-in-Publication Data
A catalog record for this book is available from the Library of Congress

Typeset in Fournier by MJ & N Gavan, Truro, Cornwall
Printed and bound by CPI Group (UK) Ltd, Croydon, CR0 4YY

Immediately afterwards, a young man in a suit came in and installed himself in the middle of the room and made a speech. No one was listening and he wasn't addressing anyone. We had to adapt to changing times, yes, to progress, and progress wasn't any old thing, but could be measured, was profitability. Innovation was important, everyone was responsible, everyone had to find a role, a style, and people mustn't stay behind, indulge in retrograde ideas and behaviour. Challenges, competition – these must be confronted. We were not the only ones in the market and we'd just have to do the best we could.

Leslie Kaplan, Mathias et la Révolution

Contents

Preface to the English Edition: Anatomy of the New Neoliberalism

Over the last decade or so, the 'end of liberalism' has regularly been announced: the global financial crisis of 2008 was presented as the last spasm in its death agony; next was the turn of the Greek crisis in Europe (until July 2015 at least), not to mention the thunderclap of Donald Trump's election in the USA in November 2016, following the Brexit referendum result in June 2016. The fact that Britain and the US, homelands of neoliberalism in the time of Thatcher and Reagan, seemed to be repudiating it, in an abrupt nationalist reaction, was symbolically striking. Since then, in October 2018, we have had the election of Jair Bolsonaro in Brazil, promising a return to dictatorship and the implementation of a neoliberal programme of a violence and scale comparable to that of Pinochet and his Chicago boys. Not only has neoliberalism survived as a system of power, but it has been strengthened. This singular radicalization is what we need to understand, and it entails appreciating the simultaneously *plastic* and *plural* character of neoliberalism. But we must go even further and grasp the meaning of the current changes in neoliberalism – in other words, the specificity of what we call the *new neoliberalism*.

Crisis as a Mode of Government

Let us first recall what the concept of neoliberalism involves, for it loses much of its pertinence when it is employed in a confused way, which it often is. It does not simply concern monetarist or austerity economic policies, or the commodification of social relations, or the 'dictatorship of financial markets'. More fundamentally, it involves a political rationality that has become global, which consists in government imposing the *logic of capital* in the economy, but also in society and the state itself, to the point of making it the form of subjectivity and the norm of existence. A radical project, a revolutionary one even, neoliberalism is therefore not to be confused with a conservatism content to reproduce established inegalitarian structures. Through the mechanism of international relations of competition and domination, through the mediation of major organizations of 'global governance' (IMF, World Bank, EU, and so on), this mode of government has over time become a veritable world system of power governed by the imperative of self-preservation.

What characterizes this mode of government is that it is fuelled and radicalized by its own crises. Neoliberalism is sustained and strengthened because it governs *through crisis*. Since the 1970s, neoliberalism has in fact been nurtured by the economic and social crises it generates. Its response is unvarying: rather than questioning the logic that prompted them, this logic must be extended and its indefinite reinforcement pursued. If austerity creates fiscal deficits, a supplementary dose is required. If competition destroys the industrial fabric or lays waste to regions, more of it must be introduced between firms, regions, cities. If public services are not fulfilling their mission, the latter must be voided of any meaning and those services deprived of resources. If tax reductions for the wealthy or corporations do not yield the anticipated results, they must be amplified, and so on and so forth. Obviously, government through crisis is possible only because neoliberalism has become systemic. Economic crises like that of 2008 are interpreted in the system's terms and elicit responses compatible with it. The 'absence of any alternative' is not simply an expression of intellectual dogmatism, but the manifestation of a systemic modus operandi on a global scale. Thanks to globalization and/or by strengthening the European Union, states have put in place rules and constraints that lead them to react in conformity with the system.

But a more recent development, which definitely warrants attention, is that neoliberalism now feeds off the negative reactions it provokes politically, that it is strengthened by the very political hostility it fans. We are living through a metamorphosis of neoliberalism – and a very dangerous phenomenon it is. Neoliberalism no longer needs its liberal or 'democratic' image, as in the good old days of what must now be called 'classical neoliberalism'. This image has itself become an obstacle to its domination. And this is possible because neoliberal government has no hesitation instrumentalizing the resentment of a broad section of the population suffering a lack of national identity and state protection, directing them against scapegoats. In the past, neoliberalism was often associated with 'openness', 'progress', 'individual liberties', and the 'rule of law'. Today, it is conjugated with the closure of borders, the erection of 'walls', the cult of the nation and state sovereignty, and a campaign against human rights, which are accused of endangering security. How has this metamorphosis of neoliberalism come about?

Trumpism and Fascism

Trump unquestionably represents a significant development in the history of global neoliberalism. This mutation does not only concern the US. It affects all those governments, increasingly numerous, which exhibit nationalist, authoritarian and xenophobic tendencies, to the point of accepting the reference to fascism, as in the case of Matteo Salvini in Italy, or military dictatorship, as with Bolsonaro. The key thing is to appreciate that such governments in no way challenge neoliberalism as a mode of power. Quite the reverse, they lighten the tax burden on the wealthiest, reduce social benefits, and speed up deregulation, particularly in financial or ecological matters. These authoritarian governments, of which the Extreme Right is increasingly a component, in reality accept the absolutist, hyper-authoritarian character of neoliberalism.

To grasp this transformation, we must avoid two errors. The older of them consists in confusing neoliberalism with 'ultra-liberalism', libertarianism, a 'return to Adam Smith', or 'the end of the state' and so on. As Michel Foucault long ago taught us, neoliberalism is a highly active mode of government that has little to do with the passive minimal state of classical liberalism. It is not the degree of state intervention, or its coercive character, that is new. What is new is that neoliberalism's fundamentally anti-democratic character, evident in the works of some of its major theoreticians, such as Friedrich Hayek, translates today into an ever more open and radical political challenge to the principles and forms of liberal democracy.

The second, more recent error consists in arguing that we are dealing with a new 'neoliberal fascism' or with a 'neofascist moment in neoliberalism'.[1] That it is (to say the least) risky, if not politically dangerous, to speak with Chantal Mouffe of a 'populist moment', and project populism as a 'remedy' for neoliberalism, is not in doubt. That it is necessary to unmask the imposture of an Emmanuel Macron, presenting himself as the only recourse against the 'illiberal democracy' of Viktor Orbán and co., is equally certain. But does this justify amalgamating 'the rise of the Extreme Right and the authoritarian drift of neoliberalism' in a single political phenomenon? Such an assimilation is manifestly problematic: how, other than in a superficial analogy, can we identify the 'total state' characteristic of fascism with the general diffusion of the market and enterprise model throughout society? While focusing on the 'Trump phenomenon' makes it possible to bring out a number of features

---

1 Eric Fassin, 'Le moment néofasciste du néolibéralisme', *Identités politiques* (blog), *Mediapart*, 29 June 2018.

of the 'new neoliberalism', it ultimately masks the latter's historical individuality. The semantic inflation of fascism certainly has critical effects, but it tends to 'drown' complex, singular phenomena in inapt generalizations, which in turn can lead only to political disarmament.

For Henry Giroux, for example, 'neoliberal fascism' is a 'specific economic-political formation' mixing economic orthodoxy, militarism, contempt for institutions and laws, white supremacism, machismo, hatred of intellectuals, and amoralism. Giroux borrows from the historian of fascism Robert Paxton the idea that fascism is based on 'mobilizing passions' that are also to be found in 'neoliberal fascism': love of the leader, hyper-nationalism, racist fantasies, contempt for what is 'weak', 'inferior' and 'foreign', disdain for individual rights and dignity, violence against opponents, and so on.[2]

While all these ingredients are indeed to be found in Trumpism, and a fortiori in Brazilian Bolsonarism, is this not to miss its specificity vis-à-vis historical fascism? Paxton agrees that 'Trump adopts several typically fascist motifs', but he perceives in him above all the more common features of a 'plutocratic dictatorship'.[3] For there are also major differences from fascism: no single party, no proscription of all opposition and dissidence, no mobilization and enlistment of the masses in compulsory hierarchical organizations, no professional corporatism, no liturgy of a secular religion,

2   See Robert O. Paxton, *The Anatomy of Fascism*, New York: Alfred A. Knopf, 2004. Cf. Henry Giroux, 'Neoliberal Fascism and the Echoes of History'; truthdig.com, 2 August 2018.

3   Robert O. Paxton, 'Le régime de Trump est une ploutocratie', *Le Monde*, 6 March 2017.

no ideal of the 'citizen soldier' totally devoted to the total state, and so on.[4] In this regard, any parallel with the late 1930s in the USA is misleading, despite Trump's adoption of the slogan 'America First' – the name given by Charles Lindbergh to the organization he championed to promote an isolationist policy against Roosevelt's interventionism. Trump has not brought to life the scenario imagined by Philip Roth, which sees Lindbergh beat Roosevelt in the 1940 presidential election.[5] It is not simply that Trump is not to Clinton or Obama what Lindbergh was to Roosevelt, and that any analogy here is shaky. While Trump jacks up the rhetoric in an 'anti-establishment' pitch to his electoral constituency, he does not seek to provoke anti-Semitic riots, unlike Lindbergh in the novel, who is directly inspired by the Nazi example. Above all, contrary to what Robert Kuttner believes, we are not living through a 'Polanyi-esque moment' characterized by the restoration of control over markets by fascist powers faced with the ravages of laissez-faire.[6] In a sense, the exact opposite is true and it is much more paradoxical. Trump aims to be the champion of entrepreneurial rationality, including in the way he conducts domestic and foreign policy. We are living the moment when neoliberalism secretes from within an original political form that combines anti-democratic authoritarianism, economic nationalism and expanded capitalist rationality.

---

4   Cf. Emilio Gentile, *Qu'est-ce que le fascisme? Histoire et interpretation*, Paris: Gallimard, 2004.

5   Philip Roth, *The Plot against America*, New York: Houghton Mifflin, 2004.

6   See Robert Kuttner, *Can Democracy Survive Global Capitalism?*, New York and London: W.W. Norton & Co., 2018.

A Major Crisis of Liberal Democracy

To understand the current mutation of neoliberalism, and avoid misconstruing it as its end, we require a dynamic conception of that mutation. Three or four decades of neoliberalization have profoundly affected society by comprehensively establishing situations of rivalry, precarity, uncertainty, and absolute and relative impoverishment in social relations. The generalized creation of competition between economies and, indirectly, between wage-earners, laws and the institutions that supervise economic activity, has had destructive effects on the condition of wage-earners, who feel abandoned and betrayed. Society's collective defences have been undermined. In particular, trade unions have lost power and legitimacy. Workplace collectives have frequently broken down under the impact of a highly individualizing form of management. Political participation has lost its meaning given the absence of a choice between significantly different options. Converted to the dominant rationality, social democracy is in the process of becoming extinct in a large number of countries. In sum, neoliberalism has engendered what Gramsci called 'monsters' through a dual process of disaffiliation from the 'political community' and re-affiliation to ethno-identitarian and authoritarian principles that challenge the 'normal' functioning of liberal democracies. The tragic thing about neoliberalism is that, in the name of the supreme reason of capital, it has attacked the very foundations of social life as they took shape and became established in the modern epoch through social and intellectual critique. To put it unduly schematically,

application of the most basic principles of liberal democracy soon meant more concessions to the masses than was
acceptable to classical liberalism. This is the true meaning
of the 'social justice' or 'social democracy' against which
the cohort of neoliberal theoreticians has never stopped
inveighing. In the attempt to make society an 'order of
competition' composed exclusively of 'economic man' or
'human capital', struggling against their fellows, the very
bases of social and political life in modern societies have
been undermined – in particular, by fuelling the resentment and anger that such a mutation is bound to induce.

Why, then, be surprised by the response of the mass
of 'losers' to the establishment of this competitive order?
Seeing their conditions deteriorate and their collective
supports and reference points disappear, they take refuge
in political abstention or a protest vote, which is primarily a call for protection against the threats to their life and
future. In a word, neoliberalism has induced a major crisis
of 'liberal-social democracy', whose most obvious expression is the rise to power of authoritarian regimes and
extreme right-wing parties supported by a broad swathe of
'national' popular classes. We have left behind the era of the
post–Cold War when it was still possible to elicit credence
in the global extension of the 'market democracy' model.
We are now witnessing, on an accelerated basis, a converse
process of 'exit from democracy', or 'de-democratization',
to adopt Wendy Brown's altogether apt term. Journalists
love to conflate Extreme Right and Radical Left in the
vast swamp of an 'anti-systemic' populism. They do not
see that the channelling and exploitation of this anger and

resentment by the Extreme Right gives rise to an even more aggressive, militarized and violent new neoliberalism, of which Trump is at once the ensign and caricature.

The New Neoliberalism

What we are calling the 'new neoliberalism' is an original version of neoliberal rationality, in that it has openly adopted the paradigm of war *against the population*. In order to legitimize itself, it relies on the anger of that same population and even invokes 'popular sovereignty', variously directed against elites, globalization, or the European Union. In other words, a contemporary variant of neoliberal power has embraced the rhetoric of national sovereignty and adopted a populist style, so as to strengthen and radicalize capital's dominion over society. Basically, it is as if neoliberalism were using the crisis of liberal-social democracy it has generated, and which it constantly exacerbates, the better to impose the logic of capital on society. To be perfected, this recuperation of anger and resentment doubtless requires the charisma of a leader capable of embodying what long remained an unlikely synthesis of economic nationalism, liberalization of economic and financial mechanisms, and a systematically 'pro-business' policy. However, today, all national variants of neoliberalism are engaged in a general transformation whose virtually pure form is supplied by Trumpism. This transformation accentuates one of the generic aspects of neoliberalism: its fundamentally *strategic* character. For (let us repeat) neoliberalism is not a form of conservatism. It is a governmental paradigm whose principle is war on the 'archaic' structures and 'backward' forces resisting the extension of capitalist rationality and, more widely, the struggle to impose a normative logic on populations that do not want it. To achieve its ends, this power uses all requisite means: media propaganda, legitimation by economic science, blackmail and lies, broken promises, the systemic corruption of 'elites', and so forth. But one of its preferred levers is still the route of 'legality', even the constitution, to render the context in which all 'actors' must play ever more irreversible. Obviously, this is an asymmetrical legality, more favourable to the interests of the wealthy classes than the rest. There is no need to resort to old-style military coups d'état to implement the precepts of the Chicago School if, as in Brazil, the political system can be bolted shut by a parliamentary and then judicial *golpe*. The latter, for example, allowed President Michel Temer to freeze social expenditure (especially on public health and higher education) for twenty years. In reality, the Brazilian case is not isolated, even if the mechanisms of the manoeuvre are more conspicuous there than elsewhere, above all since Bolsonaro's victory as the end result of the process. The phenomenon, whatever its national variants, is a general one: it is within the formal framework of the representative political system that anti-democratic devices of formidable corrosive efficacy are put in place.

A Civil War Government

Neoliberal logic contains a declaration of war on all forces of resistance to 'reforms' at all levels of society. The terminology used by rulers is not misleading. The whole population must feel itself mobilized by the 'economic war', and reforms of labour law and social protection are implemented precisely in order to encourage universal enlistment in this war. Symbolically and institutionally alike, a major change has occurred when the principle of competitiveness has become a quasi-constitutional principle. Since we are at war, the principles of the separation of powers, human rights and popular sovereignty possess a merely *relative* value. In other words, 'liberal-social democracy' is progressively tending to be hollowed out, becoming the juridico-political envelope of a war government. All those opposed to neo-liberalization are positioned outside the legitimate public sphere; they are unpatriotic, if not traitors.

The strategic matrix of economic and social changes, closely approximating to a naturalized civil war model, coincides with a different, more authentically military and police tradition, which makes 'national security' the government's top priority. Neoliberalism and the security state happily coexisted early on. The undermining of the public freedoms of the *Rechtsstaat*, and the concomitant extension of police powers, intensified with the 'war on crime' and 'war on drugs' from the 1970s. But it is especially since the declaration of the 'war on terror', in the aftermath of 11 September 2001, that we have seen the deployment of a set of measures and apparatuses openly violating the rules of the protection of liberties in a liberal democracy, to the point of enshrining in law mass surveillance of the population, imprisonment without due process, and the systematic use of torture. For Bernard E. Harcourt, this model of government, which consists in 'making war on all citizens', derives directly from the counter-insurgency strategies perfected by the French army in Indochina and Algeria, transmitted to US specialists in the fight against communism and applied by their allies, particularly in Latin America and South-East Asia. Today, 'counter-revolution without revolution' (as Harcourt dubs it) aims by any means to defeat a ubiquitous internal and external enemy that preferably takes the shape of the jihadist, but which can assume many other forms (students, ecologists, farmers, young Blacks in the USA or youth in French suburbs, and perhaps especially today illegal immigrants, Muslims in particular). And to prosecute this war against the enemy, it is important for the government to militarize the police and collect a mass of information on the population to forestall any possible rebellion.[7] In sum, state terrorism is once again advancing, while the 'communist threat' that served to justify it during the Cold War has disappeared.

The fusion of these two dimensions – the radicalization of neoliberal strategy and the military paradigm of counter-insurgency warfare starting from the same civil war matrix – is the principal accelerator of the exit from democracy today. And this marriage is only possible because of the skill with which a number of right-wing leaders, but also left-wing leaders, have undertaken to channel the resentments and hatred of elective enemies in populist style, while promising the masses order and protection in exchange for support for their authoritarian neoliberal policy.

---

7 Bernard E. Harcourt, *The Counterrevolution: How Our Government Went to War against Its Own Citizens*, New York: Basic Books, 2018.

The Neoliberalism of Macron

But is it not an exaggeration to put all forms of neoliberalism in the same basket of a 'new neoliberalism'? There are very severe tensions at a global or European level between what must be called different national types of neoliberalism. Doubtless Justin Trudeau, Angela Merkel or Macron cannot be equated with Trump, Erdoğan, Orbán, Salvini or Bolsonaro. Some remain attached to a form of supposedly 'fair' trade competition, while Trump has decided to change the rules of the competition by transforming it into a trade war in the service of American greatness ('making America great again'). Some still pay lip service to human rights, the separation of powers, tolerance and equal rights for individuals, while others pay them no heed. Some aim to have a 'humane' attitude towards migrants (very hypocritically in some instances), while others have no hesitation in repressing and expelling them. We must therefore grant a diversification of the neoliberal model. Macronism is not Trumpism, if only because of the pertinent national political histories and structures. Macron presented himself as a bulwark against the extreme right-wing populism of Marine Le Pen, as the seeming antithesis of it. Yet Macron and Le Pen, while not identical, are in reality perfectly complementary. One plays the bulwark while the other dons the garb of the scarecrow, allowing the former to present himself as the guarantor of liberties and human values. If needs be, as is the case today in the run-up to the European elections, Macron sets about artificially widening the putative cleavage between the supporters of 'liberal democracy' and partisans of 'illiberal democracy' Orbán-style, so as to make people believe that the EU in and of itself is on the side of liberal democracy.

However, insufficient attention has perhaps been paid to Macron's *populist style*, which might have seemed a sheer masquerade on the part of a pure product of the French political and financial 'elite'. Denunciation of the 'old world' of political parties, rejection of the 'system', ritual invocation of the 'people of France' – all this was superficial enough, grotesque even. Yet it attested to a method characteristic of the new neoliberalism: recuperation of anger at the neoliberal system. But Macronism did not enjoy the political space to play this tune for long. He was soon seen for what he is and what he does. In line with previous French governments, but more explicitly (or less shamefacedly), in the name of Europe he has combined the crudest, most cynical economic violence against wage-earners, pensioners, civil servants and welfare claimants with systematic police violence against demonstrations by opponents (as we saw at Notre-Dame-des-Landes), but also against migrants. Even the most peaceful of trade-union or student demonstrations are systematically repressed by a super-equipped police force, whose new manoeuvres and forceful techniques aim to terrorize those who protest and frighten the rest of the population. The case of Macron is most interesting for completing our picture of the new neoliberalism. Pushing identification of the state with the private enterprise to the point of wishing to make France a 'startup nation', he continues to centralize power in his hands and goes so far as to promote a constitutional change that would weaken parliament in the name of 'efficiency'. The difference with Nicolas Sarkozy here is clear: while Sarkozy multiplied provocative statements even as he affected a 'relaxed' style in the performance of his duties, Macron intends to restore all the lustre and solemnity to the post of president. He thus combines enterprise despotism with curbing the institutions of representative democracy in favour of the executive. Reference has legitimately been made to 'Bonapartism' in his regard, not only on account of the way he took power by sweeping away the old parties of government, but also because of his express contempt for all counter-powers. The novelty he has introduced into the old Bonapartist tradition is precisely a veritable entrepreneurial governance. Macronism is a *managerial Bonapartism*.

The authoritarian, vertical aspect of his manner of government fits perfectly in the framework of a new, more violent and more aggressive neoliberalism, in accordance with the war on enemies of national security. Was not one of Macron's most emblematic measures the introduction into the ordinary law in October 2017 of the 'exceptional' measures of the state of emergency introduced following the attacks of November 2015?

Recourse to the Law against Democracy

A 'Polanyi-esque moment' – i.e., a genuine fascist solution – cannot be excluded in the West, whether in its centre or periphery, especially if a new crisis comparable in scale to that of 2008 erupts. The arrival of the Extreme Right in power in Italy is an additional warning. Meanwhile, until further notice, we are dealing with an *exacerbation of neo-liberalism* that combines maximum freedom for capital with increasingly profound attacks on liberal-social democracy, whether in the socio-economic or judicial and policing spheres. Should we simply adopt the critical commonplace that 'the state of exception has become the rule'? Against the argument, originating with Carl Schmitt and adopted by Giorgio Agamben, of the 'permanent state of exception', which assumes suspension pure and simple of the rule of law, we must set the observable facts: it is via the *legalization* of measures of economic and policing warfare that the new neoliberal power has been installed and crystallized. Since social, economic and political crises are permanent, it is for legislation to establish the permanently valid rules that allow governments to respond to them at any point and even forestall them. Thus it is that crises and emergencies have facilitated the birth of what Harcourt calls a 'new state of legality', which legalizes what were hitherto only emergency measures or conjunctural responses in economic or social policy.[8] Rather than a state of exception pitting rules and exception against one another, what we have is a gradual, rather subtle transformation of the *Rechtsstaat* that has integrated into its legislation the situation of dual warfare, in the economic and policing spheres, into which governments have led us. In truth, the rulers are not at a complete loss when it comes to legitimizing this transformation intellectually. Neoliberal doctrine had already developed the principle of such a conception of the *Rechtsstaat*. Thus Hayek explicitly subordinated the *Rechtsstaat* to the 'law':

8   Harcourt, *The Counterrevolution*, p. 213ff.

to his mind *law* referred not to any particular rule, but exclusively to the kind of rules of conduct that are equally applicable to all, including public figures. What specifically characterizes law is therefore the formal universality that excludes any form of exception. Consequently, the genuine *Rechtsstaat* is the 'material *Rechtsstaat*' which requires that state action be subject to a rule applicable to all by dint of its formal character. It is not enough for some action by the state to be authorized by current legality independently of the type of rules to which it pertains. In other words, it is a question of producing not a system of exception, but a system of rules prohibiting exception. And as the economic and policing war is interminable, and demands ever more measures of coercion, the system of laws that legalize measures of economic and policing warfare is extended beyond all bounds. To put it differently, there is no check on the exercise of neoliberal power by the law precisely in so far as law has become the preferred instrument for neoliberalism's struggle against democracy. The *Rechtsstaat* is not abolished from without, but destroyed from within to make it a weapon of war on populations in the service of the powerful. Macron's draft law on pension reform is exemplary in this regard. In accordance with the requirement of formal universality, its principle is that one euro contributed assigns exactly the same right to all, whatever their social circumstances. In accordance with this principle, it is therefore impermissible to take account of the arduousness of working conditions when it comes to calculating pension points. Once again, the difference between Sarkozy and Macron leaps to the eye: whereas the former had law after law adopted without subsequent application orders, the latter is very concerned with applying laws. This is where the difference between 'reforming' and 'transforming', dear to Macron, is to be found: the neoliberal transformation of society requires continuity of application over time and cannot make do with the impact of announcements without any follow-up. Moreover, this modus operandi possesses an incalculable advantage: once the law has been adopted, governments can evade their share of responsibility on the grounds that they are simply 'applying the law'. Basically, the new neoliberalism is the continuation of the old for the worse. The *comprehensive normative framework* that enlists individuals and institutions in an implacable war logic increasingly restricts and defeats capacities for resistance by deactivating the collective. The anti-democratic nature of the neoliberal system largely accounts for the endless spiral of the crisis and the acceleration before our eyes of the 'de-democratization' process whereby democracy is emptied of its substance without being formally abolished.

Introduction:
From Bad to Worse

We write this book with a sense of urgency. Things are moving fast. We are witnessing a significant *acceleration* in the economic and securitarian processes that are profoundly transforming our societies, as well as the political relations between rulers and ruled. Regardless of whether this change of speed is fuelled by the financial crisis, the debt crisis in Europe, the arrival of Syrian refugees, terrorist attacks, or the electoral rise of the Extreme Right, the main direction is the same. We are dealing with an acceleration in the *exit from democracy*. It has two complementary aspects: the recharged power of the oligarchic offensive against citizens' social and economic rights; and the proliferation of security apparatuses targeting their civil and political rights. These two aspects do not pertain to different 'policies' – 'liberal' and 'securitarian', respectively – between which rulers can choose, depending on circumstances and elections. Need we remind readers? The formula trotted out today –

'security is the foremost freedom' – featured in the report *Réponses à la violence* issued by the Committee of Inquiry into Violence, chaired by Alain Peyrefitte – a report that lay behind the February 1981 Security and Liberty law drafted by the same Peyrefitte, who had become justice minister. In the guise of the Giscardian Right, French neoliberalism played a pioneering role in combining 'advanced liberalism' with state securitarianism.

Peyrefitte's formula has the advantage of masking the nature of the combination by identifying security as the *number one* freedom, without further ado. In reality, it is 'freedom' of competition – unremitting, unbridled competition between actors – that requires the reinforcement of 'security', or, rather, generates the 'securitarian' as a precondition of its operation.[1] For we must distinguish between *sûreté* [safety] and the *sécurité* promoted by securitarian logic. If *sûreté* is one of the fundamental rights recognized by the 1789 Declaration, it is because it is a guarantee intended to protect the citizen from arbitrariness – first and foremost, arbitrary conduct on the part of the state. And if Montesquieu and Rousseau can identity 'political liberty' with '*sûreté*',[2] it is precisely because they do not make it a

---

1   Foucault demonstrated the point very clearly: security strategies are liberal governmentality's 'other face and its very condition' (*The Birth of Biopolitics: Lectures at the Collège de France 1978–1979*, ed. Michel Senellart, trans. Graham Burchell, New York and London: Palgrave Macmillan, 2008, p. 65). What is true of liberalism, which promotes free trade and free markets, is a fortiori true of neoliberalism, which promotes freedom of competition. There is thus a whole 'interplay between security and liberty', involving a trade-off between security and liberty in accordance with the dangers spawned by divergent interests.

2   Montesquieu in Book XII, Chapter 2 of *The Spirit of the Laws* and Rousseau in Book II, Chapter 4 of *The Social Contract*.

freedom, albeit the first. There is therefore nothing neutral about the triumph of the securitarian under neoliberalism: whereas *sûreté* protects persons from abuses of state power, the securitarian pertains exclusively to the state.[3] In fact, this is a basic orientation that has prevailed for more than three decades and is intensifying with the rapid succession of 'crises'. It derives from a unique form of rationality: neoliberalism. By concentrating real power in the hands of the most powerful economic actors at the expense of the mass of citizens, neoliberal political reason makes people insecure and disciplines them, deactivates democracy, and fragments society.

By 'neoliberalism' we therefore understand something very different from the standard sense of the term. We mean not the set of doctrines, tendencies or actors – very diverse and, in some respects, opposed – filed by political and economic history under that overly broad heading, or economic policies deriving from a desire to undermine the state in favour of the market, but instead what we have ana-lysed as a 'world-reason' whose main characteristic is that it extends and imposes the logic of *capital* on the totality of social relations, to the point of making it the very form of our lives.[4] The most diverse ideologies adapt perfectly well

---

3   From this point of view, constitutionalization of the state of emer-gency, or the inscription of its content in an ordinary law, by prioritizing the imperative of security over that of judicial control, is highly injurious to citizens' *safety [sûreté]*.

4   See Pierre Dardot and Christian Laval, *La nouvelle raison du monde*, Paris: La Découverte/Poche, 2010; abridged English edition trans. Gregory Elliott as *The New Way of the World: On Neoliberal Society*, London and New York: Verso, 2013. Such is the core of the El Khomri 'labour law' (2016): nothing less than subordination of the rights of persons to the sacrosanct

to this rationality or, rather, actively assist it. The example of the AKP government in Turkey is very revealing in this regard. We are familiar with the re-Islamization of society single-mindedly pursued by Erdoğan over the last few years. But the same leader declared in 2015 that 'I would like this country to be managed like a large company';[5] put through a law on higher education in the same year that completely reorganized universities on the basis of competition and performance; and restructured the health system, with the largest slice of the cake going to private hospitals. The point is not that neoliberalism is compatible with Islam, or that Islam has consciously reformed its content to adapt to globalization. It is that neoliberalism is capable of enlisting in its logic Islamist conservatism, as well as other ideologies competing with it in the market of 'cultural identities'. The real power of a global rationality consists in this capacity.

Consequently, we must examine the *systemic* character of the neoliberal phenomenon in the light of what has occurred since the crisis of 2008. For it renders any policy reorientation difficult, or impossible, even though current policies reproduce the factors underlying the crisis and make the social situation worse. In reality, we are no longer dealing with an open context where different 'policy options' might have their place – for example, social-democratic policies in the more traditional sense of the term. We are dealing with a global neoliberal *system* that no longer tolerates any

---

'needs of enterprises', disciplining individual existence in line with those needs.

5   Statement of 15 March 2015, trtturk.com/haber/.

deviation from implementing a programme of radical transformation of society and individuals. This is certainly not
a *one-party* system, but it is without doubt a *one-political-
rationality* system. And competition between parties, like
alternation between Right and Left, must be aligned with
this sole form of reason. This is what we need to begin thinking through if we are to abolish an infernal dynamic and free
ourselves from the 'iron cage' in which we are imprisoned.

The situation is fraught with danger – and not just in
France. There is no longer *anything* in common between
what the majority of people experience, feel and think and
what the powerful in their 'sensory isolation tank' perceive
and understand of the situation – not even the minimum
that makes it possible to share experience. And this is the
greatest danger. Today, no 'educational' communications
campaign can restore legitimacy to oligarchic groups. In
the absence of any credible alternative response emerging
from struggles at the base of society, an enormous fund of
resentment is forming and accumulating, which is expressed
in the urge to 'overturn the table', in apathetic withdrawal
or in xenophobia. The electoral success of extreme right-
wing parties like the National Front is a direct consequence
of the neoliberal consensus 'on high' and its rejection 'down
below'. It is perfectly possible that austerity in Europe is
leading towards a political catastrophe. The victory of neo-
fascism has now become a possibility to be reckoned with.
No one can say: 'We didn't know.'

The political authorities seem unhinged. Faced with
the neoliberal system's profound impact on society, with
the 'war of identities' that increasingly divides it, further

aggravating the logic of competition, they seem incapable of imagining any response other than the reinforcement of police powers, arbitrary imprisonment or generalized surveillance – in a nutshell, erosion of the *Rechtsstaat*.[6] History has taught them nothing. However, there is grave danger when states describing themselves as 'democracies' dust off the judicial arsenal of tyrannies that proclaim themselves such. But what is even more disturbing, if possible, is the 'nationalist rage' coursing through Europe and France, contaminating Right and Left alike. The *'rabies nationalis'* evoked by Nietzsche in July 1888 remains the 'last malady of European reason', which resulted in the well-known calamities of the twentieth century.[7] However – an aggravating factor – whereas in the 1880s, nationalism meant asserting the sovereignty of young nations following the 1848 insurrections, contemporary nationalism is predominantly motivated by a desire to restore a lost sovereignty, fantasized in nostalgic, reactive fashion.

We know various forms of resistance exist. We have analysed alternative practices. We have identified the operative principle of struggles and experiments holding out the promise of 'another world'.[8] For us there is nothing inevitable about the accelerated neoliberalization of societies. The

---

6   At a time of confusion, it should be recalled that the *Rechtsstaat* is not so much a particular form of the state as a limitation of the state, whatever its form, by the superior authority of the law.

7   Friedrich Nietzsche, *Œuvres philosophiques complètes*, vol. XIV, *Fragments posthumes*, Paris: Gallimard, 1977, p. 280. '*Rabies nationalis*' means 'nationalist rabies'.

8   See Pierre Dardot and Christian Laval, *Commun. Essai sur la révolution au XXIe siècle*, Paris: La Découverte/Poche, 2015 (English translation forthcoming, London: Bloomsbury).

immediate reasons for it lie in the current disparity in power between a dominant logic and a minority logic. The dominant logic thrives on crises and, in turn, is forever nurturing 'morbid phenomena', pitiless, terrifying 'monsters' that aim to subject society to ethno-identitarian principles.[9] These 'Monsters' are all the more alarming in that they grow with social anger and fuel one another with their mutual hatred. On the other side, the minority logic of the commons has yet to find mass expression, institutional frameworks or a political grammar. We are still only in the early stages of a new revolutionary configuration. And this delay is a cause for concern. The so-called 'radical' or 'critical' Left is flailing and sometimes in retreat. It may even capitulate to enemy forces, like Syriza in Greece in 2015.

In any event, slogans are not enough. A weakness of the critical Left is that it has made do with ready-made formulae, summary denunciations and sterile incantations. 'Ultra-liberalism', 'neoliberal totalitarianism', and 'capitalism' reduced to a single system of production are completely inappropriate concepts for a web of self-reinforcing processes that demand more detailed analysis. The old recipes of nation-statism are inoperative, even when, in a dangerous slippage, they do not resort to the rhetoric of the Right.[10] What is needed is to account for neoliberal radicalization in all its complexity and diversity. This involves understanding

---

9   Antonio Gramsci, *Selections from the Prison Notebooks*, ed. and trans. Quintin Hoare and Geoffrey Nowell Smith, London: Lawrence & Wishart, 1971, p. 276 (Notebook 3, §34).

10   On this point, see the clarification by Luc Boltanski and Arnaud Esquerre in *Vers l'extrême. Extension des domaines de la droite*, Paris: Dehors, 2014.

how the multiform crisis we are experiencing, far from being a check, has become a method of governing. In and through its effects of insecurity and destruction, neoliberalism is continually fuelling and reinforcing itself. Endeavouring to understand how – such is the ambition of this book.

1
Governing by Crisis

There is a Greek tale that shines a bright light on the present: it is a comedy by Aristophanes, performed in 388 BCE, entitled *Plutus*. The person referred to by this name is none other than the god of wealth and money, the 'god of dosh'.[1] He is cast as an old man in rags, blinded by Zeus, wandering the roads. Whereas Plutus is invariably represented as blind because he distributes wealth randomly, to rich and poor alike, the character in this play reserves his beneficence exclusively for people who are wealthy, if not swindlers and miscreants. Cured of his infirmity by the god Asclepius's treatment, he promises abundance to all. Well may 'Penia' (Poverty) object that if all poor people became rich, there would be no one left to work: the promise of universal wealth is more powerful. Everyone celebrates Plutus being

---

1 The phrase is our equivalent of one from Michel Host, translator of a French version of the play under the title *Ploutos, le dieu du fric*, Paris: Mille et une nuits, 2012.

cured. The play ends in a kind of 'inverted apotheosis':[2] to a dance rhythm and in torchlight, a solemn procession makes its way to the Acropolis to install Plutus in the Temple of Athena and the City.

Oligarchy against Democracy

In Plutus's triumph the comedy discloses a veritable 'topsy-turvy world'.[3] For the god of dosh to be consecrated guardian of the goddess's sanctuary is something that undermines the very foundations of the *polis*. The latter was constituted by the consecration of Athena's supremacy over private powers – the great aristocratic families in thrall to the terrible *lex sanguinis*. It is these very powers that are relegated to an altar located below the Acropolis. Suffice it to say that the goddess has a very strong bond with the *polis*. She is not just one divinity among others. As Hegel puts it, Athena the goddess is Athens the *polis*, or the real spirit of citizens as it lives in and through the institutions of democracy.[4] The reversal dramatized by Aristophanes (Plutus at the top of the Acropolis) indicates that what the cult of money and a frantic desire for wealth affect is the very heart of political democracy. If everyone ends up succumbing, it is because the poor are promised wealth spread universally, not blindly reserved for the rich and reprehensible.

---

2   Ibid., p. 125.
3   Ibid., p. 108.
4   G. W. F. Hegel, *Lectures on the Philosophy of World History: Introduction – Reason in History*, trans. H. B. Nisbet, Cambridge: Cambridge University Press, 1984, p. 103.

Reading these pages written 2,600 years ago, it is difficult not to think of Greece's fate today. For several years, its governments, whether willingly subservient or seeking to resist before finally caving in, have striven to satisfy the inexhaustible thirst of the god of financial markets – a Plutus long completely freed from the limits of cultivating the land and, indeed, from any real production, and solely concerned to endlessly increase the costs of his own upkeep. So much so that some architects of the Troika's privatization plans could envisage auctioning off the Parthenon itself.[5] In this sense, neoliberalism is the inversion realized; it really is the 'topsy-turvy world' invoked by Aristophanes. The financialization of the economy is the direct result of neoliberal policies. Through financial profit, investment funds and large banks corner a growing share of the wealth produced by the 'real' economy. Far from being a perversion or a form of parasitism, financialization must be considered as a set of power relations wherein societies and their institutions, like nature and subjectivities, are subjected to the law of accumulation of financial capital.

But, some may object, why should democracy be threatened by this autonomization of money, now abandoned to its overweening self-confidence (*hybris*)? And why should it die from the promise of universal wealth dangled before the poor by Plutus? On account of the universal corruption this is bound to produce? What, then, is to be understood by 'democracy' – the power (*kratos*) of the people (*demos*)? Very simply put, the word *kratos* means superiority or victory in a war against internal enemies as well as external

5 Aristophanes, *Ploutos*, p. 132.

ones. It can also signify the triumph of an opinion in an assembly. But it always involves a victory won in a confrontation. Thus, in the *polis* it is 'a word of ill repute', which democrats themselves are loath to use because it suggests that the power of the people is not power exercised by the people as a whole, but proceeds from a victory over the oligarchical 'party' by the popular 'party'.[6] If this is so, it is because, once in power, democrats themselves succumb to the 'fantasy of a *polis* one and indivisible' and endeavour to stamp out the internal war to which they owe their position. Such war is appropriately termed *stasis* – a word that in Greek means both 'position' or 'standing position' and violent insurrection or 'sedition'. That the pejorative sense of 'sedition', even open civil war, ended up prevailing cannot obscure the fact that, in a polity based on popular participation, any political position – indeed, politics as a whole – was in a sense 'seditious'.[7] So today we must recall the original meaning of the word 'democracy': not peaceful conflict management via consensus, but *power conquered by one part of the polity in a war against the oligarchic enemy*.

Does such power define a specific political regime? As regards the constitutional history of Athens, this regime was established in 403 BCE. Henceforth the people 'made themselves supreme in all fields; they run everything by decrees of the *Ekklesia* and by decisions of the *Ekasteria* in which the people [*ho demos*] are supreme [*ho*

---

6   Nicole Loraux, *La Cité divisée*, Paris: Payot, 2005, pp. 67–8. The term 'party' does not have the modern sense of a structured political party here, but refers to a section or camp within the *polis*.

7   Moses Finley, *Politics in the Ancient World*, Cambridge: Cambridge University Press, 1983, p. 106; Loraux, *Cité divisée*, p. 22.

kraton]'.[8] In a more conceptual sense, *demokratia* is the name of the regime where power is exercised by the mass of the poor, unlike oligarchy, where power is held by the wealthy minority: 'Wherever men rule by reason of their wealth ... that is an oligarchy, and where the poor rule, that is a democracy.'[9] This remarkable definition of democracy, generally omitted from the list of scholarly senses of the term,[10] makes social content, rather than number, the essential criterion. That Plutus is installed in the Acropolis by a majority of citizens, as in Aristophanes' comedy, makes no difference and does not turn an oligarchy into a democracy. A regime where a majority composed of the wealthy exercises power should not be termed a 'democracy', any more than a regime where a minority of poor people rules should be called an 'oligarchy'.

Here, the people or *demos* is not identified with a large number, or even with the totality of citizens, but with the mass of the poor, so that in and of its very essence democracy consists in the power of the poor. Similarly, oligarchy does not consist in the power of a small number (the 'few' or *oligoi*), but essentially in that of the rich (*poroi*). To which it should be added that 'democracy' designates a 'skewed' constitution: in it, the poor rule with an eye to their own benefit as poor people, not with a view to the common

---

8   Aristotle, 'The Constitution of Athens', in *The Politics* and *The Constitution of Athens*, ed. Stephen Everson, Cambridge: Cambridge University Press, 1996, p. 242.

9   Aristotle, 'The Politics', Book III, §8, in *The Politics* and *The Constitution of Athens*, p. 72.

10   With the notable exception of Wendy Brown, who recalls that, for Aristotle, democracy is 'rule by the poor' (*Undoing the Demos*, New York: Zone Books, 2015, p. 19).

good. Only government *of* the poor *for* the poor warrants the term.

The irreplaceable merit of this contrast between democracy and oligarchy on the basis of social interests is that it starkly reveals, if only negatively, the *oligarchic* essence of 'neoliberal governance' and its ferocious opposition to democracy construed as 'sovereignty of the masses'. Strictly speaking, this form of governance does not represent a new 'political regime' to be added to the traditional classification, but a hybrid mode of exercise of power consisting in rule *by* a small number or elite, in the sense of an expertocracy, and *for* the wealthy, in the sense of its social purpose. This is what we wish to analyse to render the strangeness of our own situation intelligible.

The Radicalization of Neoliberalism

It is amazing that people are not more astonished by the reinforcement of the logic that generated one of the worst crises since that of 1929. And while the latter led to profound political and doctrinal challenges, nothing of the sort has occurred since 2008. In a celebrated article of July 2008 on the 'end of neoliberalism', Joseph Stiglitz echoed Keynes's famous text *The End of Laissez-Faire*, written in 1926.[11] With this comparison, he suggested that the 1930s scenario was in the process of repeating itself. We know how things

---

11   James Galbraith among others claimed that the Reaganites' governmental doctrine foundered with the financial crisis and disappeared from the academic and political scene: *The Predator State: How Conservatives Abandoned the Free Market and Why Liberals Should Too*, New York: Free Press, 2008.

turned out. Neoliberalism, while widely discredited among ever broader swathes of the population, while provoking multifaceted resistance, was *radicalized* under the cloak of the crisis. It did not merely show resilience. Frustrating the most optimistic prognoses, it did not collapse, did not give way to a new mode of regulation. It did more than survive: it *grew stronger by radicalizing itself.* The 2008 crisis, which for many should have ushered in a *post-neoliberal moderation,* facilitated a *neoliberal radicalization.* In a remarkable essay entitled *The Strange Non-Death of Neoliberalism,* the British sociologist Colin Crouch posed the key question: why did neoliberalism emerge from the crisis stronger than ever?[12] Neoliberal radicalization is one of the most striking phenomena of the present. Its maxim? The worse things go, the more they must go on. Lower taxes for the wealthiest and their counterpart – increases for the majority – are not to be abandoned by governments just because they have not delivered the promised results. On the contrary: the same course must be maintained, because those reductions and increases were insufficiently large.

Let us briefly recall a few facts. The financial crisis of 2008 choked off growth, increased unemployment, and led to a significant loss of wealth: 23 per cent of eurozone GDP and 10 per cent of global GDP. It brought about a spectacular increase in government debt: in France, it rose from 64 per cent of GDP in 2007 to 82 per cent in 2010, and in the USA

---

12 Colin Crouch, *The Strange Non-Death of Neoliberalism,* Cambridge: Polity Press, 2011. Crouch borrows his title from a book published in 1936 by George Dangerfield, *The Strange Death of Liberal England,* which deals with the crisis of classical liberal ideas and doctrines in the 1920s.

from 65 per cent to 93 per cent; on the global scale, it swelled from 53 per cent of GDP to 70 per cent, or an increase of 54 per cent between 2007 and 2011. The member-states of the European Union mobilized 4,500 billion euros, or 37 per cent of GDP, to avert the collapse of the banking system.[13] While the final cost of the rescue package was much lower, let us note the size of the sums that had to be made available to avoid the abyss.

Eight years after the onset of the crisis, inequalities are on the rise, capital volatility is just as marked, the sacrifices required of the least well-off multiply, the state of the labour market continues to deteriorate, trade unions are weak, the Left is in pieces, what remains of social democracy is in its death throes in many countries and the Extreme Right has the wind in its sails. Europe is fragmenting, splitting apart, becoming discredited. Xenophobia is spreading; political and climate refugees die in the sea and on the roads; countless lives are wrecked by unemployment. Meanwhile, share prices have reached new heights before falling back; derivative products have proliferated; bonuses are on the rise again; shadow banking, which conducts credit operations in the utmost obscurity, has taken over from classical banks; and hedge funds, on the lookout for any prospect of quick profits in markets, have carved out a sizeable role alongside institutional investors. The global financial system is still threatened by the bursting of eminently foreseeable bubbles: the 'weapons of mass destruction' (Warren Buffett) that are derivative products circulate freely; central

---

13   ATTAC & Basta!, *Le Livre noir des banques*, Paris: Les Liens qui libèrent, 2015, p. 21.

banks have injected 13,000 billion dollars to no effect other than enriching private banks and fueling new bubbles.[14] Tax havens, where 20–30,000 billion dollars evading any taxation are parked, prosper as never before, eluding even the most feeble control and supervision. Finance, real estate and the political world continue to live in close symbiosis. Not since the nineteenth century, with its shady bankers and robber barons, has money made government policy so subservient to its dictates. The political and economic oligarchies have imposed a solution to the crisis: getting the great mass of wage-earners and pensioners to reimburse the sums injected to save the financial system from collapse and restart capital accumulation. Populations are thus plundered on a gigantic scale to repay a debt they never contracted. This truly is the 'topsy-turvy world' invoked by Aristophanes, but one that has *become a system*.

Crisis as a Method of Government

In these conditions, crisis fuels crisis in an endless spiral. The radicalization of neoliberalism largely consists in this logic of the self-feeding or, to be more exact, *self-aggravation* of crisis. If the capitalist economies of the 'centre' have become at once more unstable and less dynamic, it is because burgeoning inequalities and precarity, bound up with increased competition and unproductive financial accumulation, block growth and prevent any drop in mass unemployment. Even

---

14 Quantitative easing, which puts billions of dollars and euros at the disposal of banks, has enabled them to escape their own downward spiral and inflate their profits in the most cynical fashion.

IMF economists now concede that growing inequalities are damaging to economic growth.[15] Rather than pursuing more egalitarian and more ecological policies that would sustain popular demand, governments, under pressure from big corporations and banks, persist with 'competition policies' in their own backyard and against their peers. These reduce the share of wages in value added, depress demand and weaken organized labour. What is striking is the destruction of any counterweight, any opposition or any stabilizer.

The more the dominant logic prevails, the more it destroys anything that might check it, the more it is reinforced in accordance with a truly infernal logic. It has undermined the collective power of wage-earners, who no longer possess the 'bargaining power' to defend institutions of social protection, their purchasing power, or labour law. It has exploited the willingness of the governmental Left to discredit all the auxiliary forces that seek to come to terms with this 'Left' (some ecologist groups, and the 'accommodating' and opportunistic fractions of the old communist parties). It has even succeeded in compromising fledgling forces like Syriza in Greece. Above all, it is everywhere engaged in undermining the very foundations of liberal democracies, even including electoral legitimacy. And this not by organizing a 'Chile-style' coup d'état, but by threatening the destruction of banks and the economy – blackmailing populations over their livelihoods.

A symbolic and political coup, executed in masterly fashion by a sizeable troupe of conformist economists and

---

15   Claire Guélaud, 'Les inégalités de revenus nuisent à la croissance', *Le Monde*, 15 June 2015; http://urlz.fr/25MK.

journalists, has transferred responsibility for the crisis of private finance to the state. The state is denounced as the cause of bank failures, public deficits and the crisis of the euro, when it was the state that created market finance in the 1980s and then contributed, as a partner, to triggering the crisis of that same finance. Swollen government debt afforded an ideal pretext for blaming excessive wage demands, a surfeit of civil servants and unaffordable state handouts. As for the disasters of financial speculation, they were no longer an issue. Hot money now circulates just as freely and causes ever more serious destabilization. The systemic banks have regained control, especially in France under a purportedly 'socialist', highly obliging government, restoring their margins thanks to fulsome policies of monetary easing that pave the way for new crises in the future. Governments' instinctive response, to rescue a toxic system, turned into a new argument for reducing social protection, lowering wages and fortifying the power of capital.

The crisis has become a veritable *method of government*, accepted as such. Since the late 1970s, the 'difficult times' announced by rulers have served as the pretext for implementing what they called 'courageous policies'. The watchword of a triumphant neoliberalism was to strike the opponent without respite: 'The trick is to keep doing outrageous things. There's no point in passing some scandalous piece of legislation and then giving everyone time to get worked up about it. You have got to get in there and top it with something even worse, before the public have had a chance to work out what's hit them.'[16] The recipe has been

16 Jonathan Coe, *What a Carve Up!*, London: Penguin, 1995, p. 313.

tested many times since. But the trial period of neoliberal governmentality (to adopt Foucault's formula) is over. Experimentation is now systematic, and crisis has become the main lever for *reinforcing* neoliberal policies. Thus, to paraphrase Churchill, it might be said that for neoliberalism, *every obstacle is an opportunity*. The disciplinary weapons of the financial markets have made it possible to pitilessly punish all transgressors of programmes of wage deflation, labour market flexibilization, privatization, and public expenditure reduction. Should a government take 'bad decisions', it would immediately be penalized by the refusal of loans or a downgrade in the credit rating awarded by the ratings agencies, which would *ipso facto* raise the interest rates payable to lenders. The Greece of Syriza is, once again, the prime example.

Governments have not hidden their submission to these 'ratings agencies', which they claimed, not so long ago, to want to subject to criteria of transparency and honesty. Quite the reverse, they have endowed these financial actors, which with state connivance have played such a prominent role in globalization, with terrifying power. They have indeed accorded them absolute power, the better to demonstrate their own powerlessness to resist them. At issue was the credibility of states in the eyes of 'markets', elevated via the 'ratings agencies' into the ultimate arbiters. What is more, European states have made themselves the direct agents of financial repression of those states that do not follow the road of absolute submission to creditors'

Such are the sentiments of the character Henry Winshaw, a Labour politician converted to Thatcherism in the 1980s.

demands. The crisis revealed that government was merely the factotum of financial capitalism. As Rawi Abdelal has so clearly shown, once states had empowered capital in the 1980s, by establishing rules of maximum liberalization, it was henceforth capital that must be protected by the state, not populations.[17] Government by crisis takes advantage of straitened circumstances for the benefit of the classes which live off capital, in one way or another. Some wish to preserve and even extend the conditions most conducive to financial profit globally; others look to increase direct pressure on wage-earners in the businesses they control.

As to the 'miracle' of government debt, it enables the transfer of resources from the poorest to the wealthiest thanks to the austerity measures implemented by states. This is the logical consequence of the policy of financing the state by borrowing on financial markets. To shift the cost of the crisis from private shareholders to taxpayers – in other words, moving from a crisis of private debt to a crisis of 'sovereign debts' – was a masterstroke of government by crisis. This method of government has been perfected and systematized. The horizon of neoliberalism has long been 'zero taxes' for big business, compensated for by transferring the whole tax burden onto poor and average households. This mechanism has had consequences of the utmost significance for accelerating financialization of the economy and its chronic instability. Insufficient household demand has been masked by private debt and the luxury

---

17   See Rawi Abdelal, *Capital Rules: The Construction of Global Finance*, Cambridge: Harvard University Press, 2007. According to the author, under the impetus of European and French zeal, we have passed from a situation of 'ruled capital' to one of 'ruling capital'.

expenditure of the wealthy classes (residential property, artworks, luxury products, large cars, yachts, etc.), fuelling so many speculative bubbles that artificially inflate GDP at the expense of universally useful public expenditure.

This system of oligarchic interests produces and reproduces the crisis, feeds off it, and finds in it the motor of its expansion. In such a world, the rulers' political methods and strategies are focused solely on enhancing competitive capacity, itself dictated by the rationality of capital which (as Marx showed) is that of *surplus*. The accumulation of value at one pole of society presupposes *less* at the other pole. Such polarization has not always been so pronounced in the history of the forms of capitalism – thanks, in particular, to the mobilization and organization of the dominated. Today, however, it has become the hallmark of neoliberal societies. The logic of *dumping* prevails in the process of generalized competition: social dumping for wage-earners; fiscal, regulatory and judicial dumping for businesses. The latter, with the support of banks and states, vie for 'fiscal attractiveness', 'competitiveness' and 'flexibility'. Behind these terms lies the wholesale victory of multinational firms, which continually lobby national or local authorities for tax breaks, subsidies, regulatory exemptions and protracted wage deflation. The consequences are the social, environmental and subjective ravages that fuel anger, despair and resignation, and which foreshadow more or less modernized political forms of fascism corresponding to the sense of abandonment felt by impoverished populations.

There are good reasons for that sense of abandonment. Neoliberalism is a vast enterprise of neo-proletarianization that takes the form, *inter alia*, of subordinating companies to shareholders (imposing new conditions of employment and new work constraints) and placing populations in thrall to the banks that finance housing, 'health capital', 'educational investment', 'old-age risk' and, of course, consumption. What we are witnessing is a new stage in *disciplining*. This no longer simply involves enclosing labour-power in factories, in the manner of the old industrial capitalism – an enclosure of the working class that is expanding dramatically in emerging countries. It also entails blackmail over jobs, financial constraints, a perfectly justified fear of inadequate resources for health, education and other services, and a climate of generalized social fear. What has been called the 'risk society' is in fact a 'society disciplined by risk'.

Crisis as a Weapon of War

We can now appreciate why the vocabulary of 'crisis' is problematic. The term is used to describe and analyse the disastrous effects of a policy of generalized crisis. But it is also employed to *justify* this policy. There is unquestionably a veritable systemic crisis. It is correct to note that the term 'crisis' has lost its original meaning – a moment of disequilibrium and disorder, calling for a decision or judgement – and has come to signify a permanent state, a regular condition rather than the disruption of an equilibrium.[18] But this remains too general. It is necessary to distinguish two things. The system is indeed in crisis and

---

18   See Myriam Revault d'Allones, *La Crise sans fin. Essai sur l'expérience moderne du temps*, Paris: Éditions du Seuil, 2012.

this crisis is as chronic as it is total; no aspect of reality is exempt, because neoliberal reason spares no dimension of human existence. But the formula also signifies that the system feeds off crisis, that it is reinforced in and through crisis. It must be remembered that neoliberal policies are not adaptations to objective logics imposed from without, like natural laws, even if they present themselves as such. Instead they strive to construct situations and intensify dynamics that *indirectly* compel governments to accept the consequences of their own previous policies. And this literally infernal logic leads to the pursuit of policies that further aggravate the situation. The hypothesis of a 'shock doctrine', advanced by Naomi Klein,[19] is only an approximation to this reality. Certainly, every natural disaster, every economic crisis, every military conflict and every terrorist attack is systematically exploited by neoliberal governments to radicalize and accelerate the transformation of economies, social systems and state apparatuses. But this strategy is not so much the product of a global conspiracy as the development, by way of self-preservation and self-reinforcement, of a normative logic that has irreversibly shaped the conduct and mentality of all political and economic 'decision-makers', and which has systematically undermined potential countervailing forces.

It is not only ideology, or some particular policy, that is neoliberal. Once the process of neoliberalization of societies and mentalities has attained a certain threshold, it is *social reality* itself which has become neoliberal. As Marx never

---

19   Naomi Klein, *The Shock Doctrine: The Rise of Disaster Capitalism*, London: Allen Lane, 2007.

tired of repeating, it is not the representation that inverts reality; it is reality itself which is inverted. It is reality that takes the form of a system of constraints on individuals, which subjects all putative 'realists' and 'pragmatists' to its iron law. This is how the 'social-democratic Left' has scuppered itself over the last thirty years. It has not simply been the victim of a reality imposed on it, prompting it to renege on its old redistributive and egalitarian ambitions. Since the 1980s, it has been to the fore in applying neoliberal rationality. French 'social democracy' played a crucial role in liberalizing finance and trade, fostering the transition to a new economic and political phase where 'capital rules'.[20]

This 'Left' has adopted the right-wing 'software program' almost in its entirety: the fetish of currency stability, the desire to reduce taxes and social expenditure, labour market flexibility and, above all, the quasi-constitutional primacy of the principle of competitiveness. A prisoner of this logic of free circulation of capital and competition, it invariably ended up acceding to the demands of capital and rejecting those of labour. Clinton, Blair, Bérégovoy, Prodi, Jospin, Schröder, followed by Hollande and Renzi, were zealous architects of neoliberal society. And it is precisely this new role of the 'Left' that explains its collapse in numerous countries, sometimes to the point of disappearing from parliament (as in Poland in October 2015), and the simultaneous rise everywhere of new conservative, nationalist, and sometimes explicitly quasi-fascist forces.

Neoliberal policies are *systematically* favourable to capital. Competition between capitals on a world scale presupposes

---

20   Cf. Abdelal, *Capital Rules.*

generalizing the policy of *competitiveness*. And, in its turn, such a policy assumes waging continuous war on every obstacle to the freedom of capitalists and the valorization of capital. The whole set of apparatuses, rules and mechanisms that the wage-earning class succeeded in imposing by its struggles and the power it acquired is the target of the 'war of the wealthy' today. Like it or not, in this 'war' the initiative is held by the forces of oligarchy and the fight is therefore asymmetrical. The term 'crisis', used for thirty or forty years to denote an objective mechanism independent of human action, conceals a political war with a multiplicity of actors, private and public, national and global. From this standpoint, politics as the exercise of power is nothing other than the form in which the class war is relentlessly waged by the politico-financial oligarchy. Its stake is the organization of society and its method is economic. It aims to transform, and some-times to destroy, the social institutions that ensure relative autonomy – individual, familial and, more broadly, collec-tive – from the labour market and subordination to capital. The main objective is ill-concealed by moralistic arguments about the 'virtue' of austerity. It consists in undermining, to the point of eliminating, everything, especially from the mid-twentieth century onwards, which enabled individuals not to be utterly dependent on capital and markets. This war has the more general effect of deactivating any capacity for autonomous collective action by society.

Neoliberalism actively works to undo democracy. It does so by imposing, little by little, piece by piece, a *comprehensive normative framework* that enrols individuals and institutions in an implacable logic, defeating any capacity to resist and fight. And this logic does not diminish over time, but grows stronger. It is the anti-democratic nature of the neoliberal system that largely accounts for the crisis spiral. The challenge to democracy takes various forms that broadly pertain to what Wendy Brown has aptly called a general process of 'de-democratization', emptying democracy of its substance without formally abolishing it. It is the parliament in Athens that votes the austerity measures which destroy the Greek economy and make debt a noose strangling society. In the absence of any room for manoeuvre, political confrontation with the *neoliberal system* is becoming inevitable. Once again, we must draw all the lessons from Greece. The issue is not whether unduly harsh policies should be softened, or whether Greece or some other country should exit the euro. The issue is much bigger and more universal. The struggle that has begun aims to regain the initiative in the class war, so as to defeat the oligarchy and establish democracy. This confrontation obviously requires a strategic analysis; and that involves returning to the neoliberal project and the way neoliberalism has imposed itself as a system.

2

The Neoliberal Project:
An Anti-Democratic Project

Before assuming the dimensions of a veritable *politico-institutional system*, neoliberalism was an ambitious *project* for renewing liberalism, conceived prior to the Second World War. From project to institutional system, the story is certainly not one of sheer continuity: a number of elements in the original project were marginalized, or even abandoned, *en route*, so that the system cannot be understood as the integral, faithful realization of the project or even as its wayward implementation. However, one thing is certain: at the heart of the project from the outset has been a fundamental *anti-democratism*. It derives from a determination to shield the rules of the market from the policy orientation of governments, by consecrating them as inviolable rules incumbent upon any government, whatever its electoral majority. The most remarkable thing is that this principled hostility towards democracy is readily justified, at least by certain neoliberal dogmatists, through a particular idea of 'democracy'.

Thus, at the height of the Greek crisis, some political leaders were to be heard solemnly recalling that democracy consisted in a government with an electoral majority honouring its commitments to European and international institutions, whatever the cost. At the same time, however, democracy was invoked 'to construct an identity between citizens and government', rendering the former jointly responsible for the debts contracted by the latter.[1] Thus the same notion – democracy – has served to assert both the responsibility of citizens for the rulers elected by them and the responsibility of those rulers to institutions that no one has elected. In both instances, what is spirited away is the rulers' responsibility *to their own electorate* – and this exclusively in favour of the responsibility of citizen-voters and their rulers *to unelected institutions*. We might wonder whether such developments, over and above the particular political context they occur in, do not involve a singular conception of democracy, sponsored by the neoliberal project. So today it is important to briefly revisit the substance of that project. For, while the latter was profoundly hostile to democracy from the outset, the neoliberal institutional system as it functions today is an inflexible, methodical system for *hollowing out democracy*, and by no means an original, unprecedented form of democracy, as some would have us believe.

---

1   Wolfgang Streeck, *Buying Time: The Delayed Crisis of Democratic Capitalism*, trans. Patrick Camiller, London and New York: Verso, 2014, p. 95.

Against 'Popular Sovereignty'

The 'democracy' attacked by neoliberalism is only very distantly related to the original sense of the word: power exercised by the mass of the poor. It is mostly a particular combination of a method for selecting rulers and a policy of redistribution in favour of the impoverished – a combination that became established after the war, under the rubric of the 'welfare state' or 'social state'. By 'democracy' we mean 'a regime which, in the name of its citizens, deploys public authority to modify the distribution of economic goods resulting from market forces'.[2] While there is 'participation', it involves citizens not in exercising power, but, much more narrowly, in selecting their leaders. In the view of supporters of this type of state, the choice in itself matters less than the social purpose of government intervention. Elected by a popular majority, leaders must govern in favour of that majority and its interests, which authorizes them to intervene in the name of social justice to rectify inequalities created by the market. The state's capacity to guarantee social rights emerges as the foundation of democracy understood as 'social democracy' or 'mass democracy'.

In complete contrast, a neoliberal like Friedrich Hayek immediately reduces 'democracy' to a technical procedure for appointing rulers: the latter are chosen by a majority of citizens and not imposed in authoritarian fashion. This reduction radically *devalues* democracy by denying it any substantive content. Far from representing a good in itself,

---

2   Ibid., p. 57.

it is nothing but a method or procedure that might very well be employed for perverse ends.[3] At issue here is the refusal to identify democracy with 'popular sovereignty', understood not as the direct exercise of legislative power by the people, but as the promotion of the will of the people to the rank of sole source of legitimacy for the rulers' activity. Very precisely targeted in that phrase is the 'absolute power' that the electoral majority is alleged to possess over the minority by dint of its direct influence upon rulers. In practice, therefore, 'popular sovereignty' must necessarily mean the rulers' submission to the will of the majority, if only via the control exercised over them by the majority's representatives in parliament.

In truth, this is not a completely new argument. It was developed by one of the founders of neoliberalism – the American journalist Walter Lippmann – in his writings on public opinion, well before the 1938 colloquium that would bear his name. According to him, the weakness and instability of democracies consisted in the fact that rulers regarded themselves as bound to follow majority opinion. To remedy this, instead of allowing them to dictate their conduct, the people's power over the choice of rulers must be restricted. Intent on systematizing the matter, Hayek went so far as to impugn the very logic of representation as it operates in the case of the legislature. With the majority's representatives making laws exclusively in its interests, the minority is oppressed by the majority via 'the omnipotence of the legislative power'. We are thus at the antipodes

---

3   Gilles Dostaler, *Le libéralisme de Hayek*, Paris: Éditions La Découverte, 2001, p. 97.

of John Locke, who made legislative power the 'supreme power'.[4] For Hayek, such power is the sign of an 'unlimited democracy' liable to degenerate into 'totalitarian democracy'. The conventional contrast between 'democracy' and 'totalitarianism' is thus negated in principle: the origin – popular choice – by no means guarantees a proper use of the power thereby conferred, for proper use depends chiefly on limiting the rulers' sphere of activity. We can see that this critique derives from a visceral mistrust of *representative democracy* – the very form favoured by classical liberalism. It is ultimately a matter of assigning non-negotiable limits to representative democracy itself.

The Pre-eminence of Private Law over Government and State

The real issue is determining the nature of these limits. They are rules of law that apply first and foremost because of their generality. We need only revisit the inaugural moment of the Lippmann Colloquium to see that the assertion of the pre-eminence of legal rules over the government was widely shared by supporters of the re-foundation of liberalism. In fact, an analogy between such rules and the highway code was taken up by several neoliberal thinkers, from Louis Rougier via Lippman to Hayek.[5] But the analogy is too rarely examined in its own right. Since the function of the highway code is to regulate the circulation of traffic on roads, it would be absurd to alter it every four or five years

---

4   See Dardot and Laval, *The New Way of the World*, pp. 141–2.
5   See ibid., pp. 56–7.

on the pretext of improving it. This is because the stability of the rules is essential to the code's operation. If they changed periodically according to traffic conditions, drivers would be unable to orient themselves in advance, which would create chaos. The same must apply to the rules of law that are to be imposed on all governments, regardless of electoral outcomes. Constituting literal 'rules of conduct' for individuals, they must therefore apply to everyone in all circumstances.

But what sort of rules of law are we talking about? There can be no objection to a simple reminder of the state's obligation to respect basic human rights – except that this reference to 'human rights' does not fit the bill. For the legal rules whose pre-eminence is asserted by neoliberalism are exclusively the rules of *private law* or *criminal law*. Such law has validity only in the sphere of private property and market exchange, where contracts assert their particular logic. The generality of legal rules is therefore not purely formal. As Hayek himself put it, 'for [the market] to function properly, it is not sufficient that the rules of law under which it operates be general rules, but their content must be such that the market will work tolerably well'.[6] That is why the rules of private law are fundamentally different from the rules of public law defining the specific organization of the state. According to Hayek once again, 'the private individual can be coerced only to obey rules of private and criminal law.'[7] A fundamental consequence is that the only

6   F. A. Hayek, *The Constitution of Liberty*, ed. Ronald Hamowy, Chicago: University of Chicago Press, 2011, p. 338.

7   F. A. Hayek, *Studies in Philosophy, Politics and Economics*, London: Routledge & Kegan Paul, 1967, p. 168.

coercion which the state can legitimately exercise is compelling individuals to respect the rules of private law. But it is difficult to see how the state could perform this role save by showing an example – in other words, imposing those rules on itself, so that 'government should be under the same rules as every private citizen.'[8] While the state is not straightforwardly equated with a private individual, it has to conduct itself *like* a private person by applying to itself the rules it imposes on private individuals. We thus obtain the neoliberal conception of the *Rechtsstaat* or 'rule of law': defined not by an obligation to respect human rights in general,[9] but by the a priori limit imposed by private law on any legislation and any government.

But how are the rules of private law to be elevated above legislature and executive? In modern Western legal thought, as it has developed since the eighteenth century, it has fallen to the *constitution* as 'basic law', or supreme judicial norm, to define the various established or 'constituted' powers within the state. According to the principle of the 'separation of powers', the state's various powers (executive, legislative, judicial) must be allocated to different bodies in order to avoid their concentration in the same hands. In the political thought of a Montesquieu, the principle assumes the sense of a 'balance' whereby 'power binds power'.[10] However that may be, such a principle in no way prejudges the role of private law, simply because it is not

---

8   Ibid., p. 175.

9   We took it in this positive sense in the introduction (see p. 6 n. 6).

10   The aim of this principle is to ensure the *safety* of citizens from arbitrary power.

for the Constitution of a state to fix a priori the relationship between the different powers and private law. In its preamble, the Constitution may well recognize property law as a basic law, but it does not have to pronounce on it as such. Private law is out of place in a political constitution.

'Demarchy' or the Constitutionalization of Private Law

Neoliberalism breaks with this conception of the Constitution. With it, the rules of private law are accorded a quite unique, utterly unprecedented status as *fully fledged constitutional norms*. Such, in short, is the project of a 'Constitution of liberty' as developed in Hayek's book of that title. According to him, the failure of all existing constitutions to guarantee individual liberty results from the inability of the separation of powers to prevent confusion between governmental and legislative power.[11] Thus he proposes a complex edifice combining three bodies: a constitutional court, a legislative assembly, and a governmental assembly. Formally, these three organs correspond to the three powers contained in any Constitution. However, they are very far from being equivalent: 'sovereignty' belongs to the constitutional court, in the sense that no power is superior to it.[12] Supreme authority is therefore possessed by a judicial power over which neither the executive power nor the legislative power can exercise any control. Of course, the constitutional court has no power to 'make' laws, since it is limited to ruling on the constitutionality of laws passed by

---

11   See Dostaler, *Le libéralisme de Hayek*, p. 99.

12   Ibid., p. 100.

the legislature. Nevertheless, it is not in the least 'checked', 'bound' or 'counterbalanced' in the exercise of its own prerogatives by the action of the other two assemblies. This is because the key issue is preventing the supremacy of the legislative power. Ultimately, it is the liberal principle of the 'balance' of powers that is sacrificed on the altar of the constitutionalization of private law. We thus have a twofold subjection, of governmental power to legislative power and of legislative power to the higher instance that oversees the constitutionality of new laws. The ideal consists in the replacement of government by people with government by law.

In itself, the formula is not new. Rousseau sought 'to place the law above man' and to 'substitute the law for man'. But he also conceived of the law as an act of the legislature and hence as an act of the popular will. In complete contrast, Hayek's intention is to cleanly sever the 'law' from the popular will, the better to elevate the former over the latter. This is because, so far as he is concerned, a genuine law is never the work of the legislature, but is always imposed on it in the form of a pre-existing custom which judges merely ratify. Laws not being 'made' by anyone, what we have is a *'nomocracy'* or 'rule of law'. This is sufficient to indicate that governing 'by' laws is not to be understood in the sense of governing 'through' laws: for the activity of governing, laws thus construed are not *means*, but exclusively *limits*. This is what grounds Hayek's distinction between 'demarchy' and 'democracy'. Whereas the term democracy has assumed the meaning of the absolute power of the people, the word demarchy signifies the limitation of the popular will by the rules of private law. There is nothing innocent about the fact that the very term demarchy replaces *kratos* by *archè*: *archè* is the word for legitimate power, whereas *kratos* is (as we have seen) the name for the power obtained by a victory over opponents – power deemed illegitimate by the oligarchy.[13] That is to say, in demarchy, *archè* belongs not so much to the people as to the 'laws', of which the supreme power in the state must be the guardian. But everyone knows that, by themselves, laws cannot govern and that it is always human beings who must govern, albeit 'by' laws.

So-called demarchy is in fact a *kratos* exercised by a minority of the wealthy and experts (the oligarchy) over the mass of the poor (the *demos*), in the name of the sovereignty of law. For, on closer inspection, far from being a mere codification of custom, the 'laws' of demarchy are determined by judges and experts utterly committed to private property, and real power belongs to them.[14] By contrast, purely representative democracy will inevitably tend to favour the 'private interests' of a contingent electoral majority, which is why the 'general interest' must be constitutionally safeguarded in the form of inviolable general rules. Neoliberalism, in its Hayekian version at least, thus makes *social* democracy an inexorable trend of *representative* democracy. If Hayek distrusts the latter, it is because it leads to the former. As Foucault saw, this in no way prevents the Hayekian state from engaging in 'legal interventionism'.[15]

---

13   Loraux, *Cité divisée*, p. 68.
14   Dardot and Laval, *Commun*, pp. 322–3.
15   Foucault, *Birth of Biopolitics*, pp. 171–2.

But it does so in the sense that it intervenes to compel all private interest groups (among them electoral majorities) to respect private law. It is in this sense that we can speak of a 'strong state'.

The Ordo-Liberal Idea of an 'Economic Constitution'

But can we entrust definition of the 'general interest' to a spontaneous process, to the extent, like Hayek, of identifying nomocracy with 'spontaneous order'?[16] Does the constitutionalization of private law not instead require active judicial construction, of which the state itself must be the agent? Such is the thesis at the heart of ordo-liberalism (from the Latin *ordo*, 'order'), or German neoliberalism. Market order, the competitive order, far from being 'spontaneous' as Hayek thought, is the effect of an 'ordering policy' (*Ordnungspolitik*) – a phrase that is to be understood in the strong sense of establishing an order. At the heart of this doctrine is thus an explicit anti-naturalism:[17] free competition can only result from a fundamental political choice by the leaders of the state, not from the 'natural course of things'. The ordo-liberal state is in no wise a minimal state restricted to regalian functions. It must protect the market economy against all kinds of abuse of power, public and private alike, by constructing an institutional framework to foster competition. Hence the importance of what the

---

16 Hayek, *Studies in Philosophy, Politics and Economics*, p. 162ff.

17 Jean-Luc Mélenchon's claim (interview in *Politis*, no. 1352, p. 6) that ordo-liberalism regards economic laws as 'laws of nature' and capitalism as a 'natural order' is a complete misinterpretation.

founder of ordo-liberalism – Walter Eucken – called an 'economic constitution'.

It must first be pointed out that such a constitution, composed of a set of basic legal rules, is conceived strictly *by analogy* with a political constitution. Just as a political constitution has the role of guaranteeing, by means of a number of basic rules, the compatibility of the individual rights vested in citizens with the general political interest, so an economic constitution must define the basic economic rules that make it possible to reconcile individual economic liberties with the general economic interest.[18] Among the constitutional principles that ground these economic liberties are private property, freedom of contract and free competition. However, public action is required to give effect to the exercise of these individual liberties. Hence the state's commitment to ensuring currency stability – a commitment that must be enshrined as such in the economic constitution. The issue is a particularly sensitive one for ordo-liberals: inflation seems to them to be predominantly the effect of the baleful influence on politicians of pressure groups defending their own interests (private banks, lobbies, trade-union monopolies). Politicians might be tempted to pursue short-term monetary policies, particularly with the approach of elections, favouring one or another interest group. The objective of controlling inflation must therefore count as a constitutional commitment

---

18   Éric Dehay, 'L'indépendance de la banque centrale en Allemagne. Des principes ordolibéraux à la pratique de la Bundesbank', in *L'Ordolibéralisme allemand. Aux sources de l'économie sociale de marché*, ed. Patricia Commun, Cergy-Pontoise: CIRAC/CICC, 2003, p. 246.

for governments of all hues, regardless of the narrow time frame of the next election.

Secondly, there follows a crucial consequence for the status of the central bank. Erecting it into a body independent of executive power will enable monetary policy to resist the pressure of private interests. The analogy between monetary order and legal order arrives on cue to justify such independence. It draws on the terminology of classical political constitutionalism by invoking the principle of the separation of powers. Following this line of argument, since democracy in principle bans political power from being both judge and party to the action, and hence a single body having the power both to define the law and to apply it, this interdiction must also apply to the currency: 'One and the same body cannot both possess regalian rights to define the unit of currency or grant the privilege of issuing it and the power to decide what quantity of money is put in circulation and to whose benefit.'[19] In order to forestall the concentration of all these powers in the hands of the executive, the government will be accorded so-called 'regalian rights', while the power to determine the quantity of money will be vested in an independent central bank. Thus, the very existence of this institution will be an obstacle to 'monetary arbitrariness'. Here we have a crucial theoretical argument: to those who object that such independence contravenes the principle of democracy, ordo-liberals respond that it alone can introduce the democratic principle of the separation of powers into regulation of the economy. Clearly, two different conceptions of democracy confront each other here:

---

19   Ibid., p. 247.

on one side, it is asserted that the electoral expression of the will of the people must ultimately prevail, including in monetary policy; on the other, the separation of powers is made the fundamental principle, applicable even to the economic system.

The key point is that, in the second conception, the central bank's independence *from executive power* entails its independence *from the electoral expression of the popular will*. In effect, as we have seen, executive power is always suspected of partiality and partisan preferences inasmuch as it derives, more or less directly, from an electoral majority. Obviously, such dependency applies equally, if not more so, to the legislative power. This last point enables us to grasp the true significance of the ordo-liberal analogy between the political constitution and an economic constitution: monetary power in the economic order is the precise analogue of legal power in the political order, so that the independence of the central bank mirrors the independence of the judiciary.[20] Examination of the Bundesbank's discourse on the occasion of certain legal proceedings reveals a highly constitutionalist conception of central-bank independence, which is clearly ordo-liberal in inspiration. Thus, in 1965 and 1979 we find the Federal Constitutional Court requesting the central bank to play the role of neutral expert, even though it (among other institutions) had been challenged in complaints from several taxpayers. In such instances, we can appreciate the unique character of the relationship between the Federal Bank and justice in Germany. In effect, while the independent central bank in the USA is

20   Ibid.

required to justify the methods it employs to fight inflation, 'the Bundesbank seems by contrast to have *a role of
arbiter approximate to that of a constitutional court.*'[21] This is
further confirmed in the aforementioned cases, when the
Constitutional Court sought the central bank's opinion on
a matter that goes to the heart of the German Constitution
– namely, currency stability. The bank is charged by the
'fundamental law' with ensuring currency stability, but
this constitutional objective involves as such the whole of
society and all the powers exercised in it. A true collective
responsibility, then, rather than the exclusive responsibility of the central bank, which it would be enough to hold
accountable for the results of its monetary policy. Instead, it
is up to the central bank to recall this collective responsibility and to identify those economic agents whose behaviour
hinders the fulfilment of a common objective.[22] Thanks to
its role as arbiter, the central bank is therefore in the position, if not of accuser, then at any rate of vigilant guardian
of the constitutionality of monetary policy.

But, it will be asked, over and above instantiation of the
separation of powers in the economic system, what is the
ultimate justification for the constitutionalization of economic objectives? In ordo-liberal doctrine, the economic
constitution, which must be transcribed into the positive
constitutional law of the state, is supposed to correspond
to a contract between the state and citizen-voters. It might
be thought that capitalism, not being a state of nature but a
social order in search of self-legitimation, invariably implies

---

21 Ibid., p. 254 (our emphasis).
22 Ibid.

a social contract in the form of a formal or informal economic 'constitution', whose terms are liable to renegotiation in accordance with the balance of forces.[23] The strength of ordo-liberalism unquestionably consists in its stress on the need for a *formal* economic constitution, setting out the non-negotiable rules of law that all parties commit themselves in advance to obey. This highly peculiar contractualism assumes that economic individuals have the same 'constitutional preferences', that is, a common interest in choosing the same system of rules – those of a market economy. It might be objected that in reality, individuals have irreducibly divergent economic interests. Ordo-liberals pre-empt this objection by distinguishing between the interests of individuals as *producers* and the interests of individuals as *consumers*. Producers cannot have common 'constitutional interests' inasmuch as they aim not at uniformly applicable rules, but at privileges of a protectionist kind. In contrast, consumers, by dint of being such, possess a common constitutional interest whatever market they are operating in. In ordo-liberal terms, it will be said that they have the same 'constitutional preference' for the process of competition. It is precisely this shared preference that defines a 'constitutional general interest' and enables a contract between consumer-voter and government.[24]

We can now understand how the economic constitution, in consecrating the order of competition, consecrates

---

23   See Streeck, *Buying Time*.

24   On this point, see Laurence Simonin, 'Le choix des règles constitutionnelles de la concurrence. Ordolibéralisme et théorie contractualiste de l'État', in Commun, ed., *L'Ordolibéralisme allemand*, pp. 68–72.

consumer sovereignty: citizen-voters are ultimately nothing other than citizen-consumers. Reconsidered from this perspective, the celebrated formula of 'social market economy' conveys its true meaning – not the mystificatory sense of a social corrective of distribution, but the one given it by its inventor, Alfred Müller-Armack, at the outset: creating a 'democracy of consumption' in and through competition.[25] From this angle, removing monetary policy from the government and entrusting it to an independent central bank displays its full significance. In effect, it is a question of facilitating control of government action by citizen-consumers. As Franz Böhm put it, such independence 'makes it possible for individuals to actually exercise their sovereignty and to control the government effectively enough that no pressure group is formed inside government organizations'.[26]

What, ultimately, should we take from this examination of the neoliberal project in its two main versions? In the first – Hayek's – the constitutionalization of private law takes the form of the ascendancy of a constitutional court over the legislative and executive powers, which are subject to its control and incapable of counterbalancing its powers. In the second – the ordo-liberals' – the same constitutionalization takes the shape of a formal economic constitution, enshrining the independence of a central bank that operates as a kind of 'economic constitutional court'. Real 'sovereignty' belongs to the constitution itself, in that

---

25   Dardot and Laval, *The New Way of the World*, p. 90.
26   Franz Böhm, 'Rule of Law in a Market Economy', quoted in Dehay, 'L'indépendance de la banque centrale en Allemagne', pp. 247–8.

it incorporates and enshrines the rules of private law. With this ordo-liberalism revives the old idea of a 'sovereignty of the Constitution' defended by the 'doctrinaires' during the Restoration and the July Monarchy. Thus Royer-Collard defended the sovereignty of the 'Charter'. As Carl Schmitt noted, the function of this curious personification of a legal norm consisted in 'elevating the statute, with its guarantees of bourgeois freedom and private property, over every political power'.[27] The issue of the actual subject of sovereignty (the people or the monarch) was thus carefully evaded.

In reality, however, sovereignty belongs less to the Constitution *in abstracto* than to the concrete persons appointed as its guardians. The originality of ordo-liberalism is that, not content with invoking major legal principles (liberty and private property), it constitutionalizes the principles of any *economic policy* (currency stability, balanced budgets, etc.). Here, once again, the sovereignty of the Constitution legitimizes the de facto sovereignty of the unelected guardians of the Constitution. In any event, whatever the form taken by constitutionalization, the crucial point lies elsewhere. Even if the principle of it is invoked for purposes of legitimation, the division of powers peculiar to liberal democracy finds itself emptied of substance in favour of a 'judicial power' limited by no 'check'. In each instance, in their different ways, what is at stake is the 'dethronement

---

27   Carl Schmitt, *Constitutional Theory*, trans. and ed. Jeffrey Seitzer, Durham, NC: Duke University Press, 2008, p. 63.

of politics'.[28] Private law, assured of escaping public deliberation and political choice, is established as the *ultima ratio* of political and social order.

---

28   F. A. Hayek, *Law, Legislation and Liberty: A New Statement of the Liberal Principles of Justice and Political Economy*, Abingdon: Routledge, 2013, p. 481.

3
Neoliberal System and Capitalism

We must stop thinking of the advent of neoliberalism in exclusively *negative* fashion – as a dismantling of existing rules, a narrowing of states' room for manoeuvre, a reduction in the sovereignty of a now drastically shrunken nation-state, or as a malfunction of liberal democracy. What must be analysed is the actual modus operandi of a *positive, original mode of power*, composed of political and financial institutions and equipped with legislative means and administrative mechanisms. This system coordinates between national spaces, contains levers for transforming societies and ensures the worldwide preservation of a certain public order. The political economy of neoliberalism is characterized not by the passivity of the political sphere, its minimal character and circumscription, but by continuous government intervention, yielding a new order. This kind of interventionism must be understood for what it is: a set of policies both conditioned and conditioning, dependent on and creative of a system.

The Disciplinary System of Competition

Neoliberalism has become an institutional and normative system in which incentivizing governmentality and disciplinary logic are mutually supportive. The neoliberal world system is inseparable from 'globalization'. As a set of rules, institutions and norms, it has facilitated the expansion of trade, the internationalization of production and the liberation of capital flows. This normative and regulatory ensemble has been constructed through international treaties, pacts and agreements and international commercial law, with the encouragement and under the supervision of international bodies (WTO, OECD, IMF, World Bank, European Commission, etc.) and private ratings agencies, whose economic policing role has continued to expand in recent years.[1]

The 'globalization of markets' is far from being some generalized chaos or anarchy, whose characteristics are exclusively negative by comparison with the preceding global public order, structured by the states' rights of sovereignty. The rules and norms underpinning globalization create a particular space, where a game unfolds that places its own constraints on actors. We must stress the strategic position occupied by multinational firms, as the main drivers of globalization. In fact, it is they who are responsible for the growing global fragmentation of production processes, which today take highly complex forms: hyperglobalization of finance, extension of outsourcing to the

---

1   On the role of the ratings agencies in the structuring of world finance, see Abdelal, *Capital Rules*, p. 162ff.

service sector, and partial relocation of certain productive activities in the vicinity of markets.[2]

The rules and norms of globalized space are, more precisely, those of competition between large financial and productive enterprises. Real competition is a ferocious struggle for market power waged by global oligopolies. We should recall that competition can take two forms: *price* and *innovation*.[3] Neoliberal capitalism typically favours innovation, while utilizing the complementary character of the two kinds of competition. This is significant given that these two modes determine two logics in organizing production that are profoundly imbricated today.[4] The first is the 'cognitive division' of labour predominant in leading sectors (biotechnology, pharmaceuticals, electronics, computer science, etc.). Here production is organized in accordance with the segmentation of relatively homogenous blocs of knowledge (such as R&D or marketing). The second is the 'Taylorist' division of labour, which has not been abolished by the first but reactivated. It is characterized by fragmentation of the production process in accordance with the imperative to minimize costs and delays, the better to compete on price.

Consequently, we must dispense with economic orthodoxy's idealized conception of competition as an interplay

---

2 El Mouhoub Mouhoud, 'Mondialisation. Les cartes rebattues', *Alternatives économiques*, no. 93, May 2012.

3 While Marx clearly identified the first form contrary to classical economics, Schumpeter conceptualized the role of the second contrary to neo-classical orthodoxy. On this point, see Pierre Dardot and Christian Laval, 'Néolibéralisme et subjectivation capitaliste', *Cités*, no. 41, 2010, pp. 38–9.

4 On these two productive logics and their imbrication, see El Mouhoub Mouhoud and Dominique Plihon, *Le Savoir et la finance*, Paris: Éditions La Découverte, 2009, pp. 63–70.

between supply and demand 'naturally' tuned to benefit the consumer, who can choose between producers. We have known since the 1930s that competition between large enterprises in real markets is 'imperfect'. Contrary to what is claimed by many of neoliberalism's critics, in practice it does not represent the application of the unrealistic neo-classical view of the atomistic market (many suppliers and many purchasers), but the application of a *revised* economic theory wherein limited competition between oligopolies, while restricting consumer choice, ultimately serves the 'general welfare' of consumers thanks to the economies of scale achieved. This revision is not nugatory: it denies one of the most basic principles of neo-classical doctrine – namely, that *individual preference* alone is rational in the market.[5] It is therefore not so much the doctrine of competition that is demoted to the rank of ideological accessory, as Colin Crouch puts it, as the idea that *all* markets should be atomistic.[6] The relevant, effective competition has, as it were, been transferred from the national to the global level.

This struggle does not end with the institutions of the capitalist economy. It involves inciting competition between labour forces, social and tax systems, political institutions and, ultimately, societies themselves. It requires that capital not be controlled or taxed, but protected through strengthened and expanded property rights, subsidized, and 'attracted' by plentiful inducements. It is not so much

---

5   However, the principle of consumer choice remains fully operational when it comes to justifying the privatization and dismantling of public services.

6   See Crouch, *Strange Non-Death of Neoliberalism*, p. 54.

the market in itself that must be free but capital, discreetly dubbed 'savings'. Such is the basis of the supply-side policies followed by all governments today in the context of globalization. But of much greater import than its doctrinal basis is that this kind of policy is imposed by the situation itself – by the functioning of competition between capitals worldwide – and that it benefits capitalists as a whole, especially the wealthiest among them. This 'system' is not a closed set of elements, but the overall effect of a set of practices, mechanisms and institutions that have progressively framed and limited the range of choice and action open to states, economic and social organizations, and individuals themselves. It is therefore nothing other than a crystallized set of norms and rules which has acquired such coherence that actors are led to act in conformity with it. This is what, in economics, is called path dependence.

The system does not merely reproduce itself. It expands and reinforces itself through the constraints it imposes on private and public actors, which normalize it, routinize it, perfect and extend it by way of repeated crises and disequilibria. This does not mean that this system of power tends to become increasingly harmonious; that everything in it becomes 'functional'; that it absorbs all differences and smothers all conflict. It simply means that the potent systemic effects influencing actors (states, enterprises, individuals, etc.) lead them to reinforce the system in which they are trapped by their conduct. This is precisely what we observe in the salience of the schema of competitiveness, which at one pole of power becomes a quasi-constitutional principle of public institutions, and at the other a model for

individual behaviour. Having become an unofficial principle of the new public law, competitiveness, as a higher norm
with which laws, reforms and government dispositions are
aligned, leads to *effectively* transforming fields of activity
and institutions by subjecting them to a logic of competition
that is designed, in and of itself, to produce competitiveness, in an unbroken circle.

More generally, the private and public actors engaged
in the struggle for economic power themselves created,
little by little, the operating rules of the competitive system
– rules that in their turn have become a variably constrain-
ing framework for those actors. A range of standard texts,
including the famous ten propositions of the 'Washington
Consensus' of the late 1980s, have served as references for
financial institutions and governments in pursuing a policy
geared to exports, openness to foreign capital, reduction
of public services, and privatization. What was initially a
summary of the drastic conditions laid down by the IMF for
agreeing loans by public and private investors in the context
of 'structural adjustment programmes' during the debt
crisis in the South has, over time, become a general normative framework conditioning access to financial markets and
more favourable borrowing terms for all countries. This
normative framework has never been the subject of a 'consensus' other than between the IMF, the World Bank and
the US Treasury. In the wake of crises, it was imposed by
the most powerful countries of the 'centre' on the countries
of the 'periphery', and then step by step on the totality of
participants in the global competitive game – especially the
member-states of the European Union.

The Neoliberal System and the 'Laws' of Capital

It will be appreciated that such a system cannot be straightforwardly deduced from the self-development of capital, inexorably generating its effects like some autonomous motor of history. The normative logic that ultimately prevailed emerged amid initially uncertain battles and policy experiments. The neoliberal society we live in is the fruit of a historical process that was not entirely programmed by its pioneers. Its elements were often assembled piecemeal, interacting with and reinforcing one another. Just as it is not the direct outcome of a homogenous doctrine, so it is not the reflection of a logic of capital creating the social, cultural and political forms conducive to it as it expands. The classical Marxist explanation ignores the fact that, far from being the crisis of capitalism *tout court*, the accumulation crisis to which neoliberalism is a response is specific, in that it is bound up with the institutional rules which had hitherto framed a certain type of capitalism. For the originality of neoliberalism is precisely that it creates a new set of rules defining not only a *different* 'regime of accumulation', but, more broadly, a *different* society. In the Marxist conception, capitalism is above all an economic 'mode of production' which, as such, is independent of law and generates the juridico-political order it needs at each stage in its self-development. Yet far from pertaining to a 'superstructure' bound to express or fetter the economic, *the juridical from the outset pertains to the relations of production*, in that it informs the economic from within. The 'economists' unconscious', as Foucault put it, which is that of every economism whether liberal or Marxist, is precisely the institution; and it is precisely to the institution that neoliberalism, especially in its ordo-liberal version, aims to restore a decisive role.

For ordo-liberalism, the point is to determine the possibility of capitalism surviving its crises – a possibility which (as we know) was yet again a subject of debate at the height of the November 2008 crisis. If we adopt a Marxist perspective, the unique, necessary logic of capital accumulation determines the unicity of capitalism: 'There can only be one capitalism since there is only one logic of capital.'[7] The contradictions manifested by capitalist society in all periods are the contradictions of capital '*tout court*'. For example, if we follow the analysis in Volume One of *Capital*, the general law of capitalist accumulation results in a tendency to the centralization of capital where competition, along with credit, is the main lever. The tendency to centralization is therefore inscribed in the logic of competition as a 'natural law' – that of 'the attraction of capital by capital'.[8] But if, like the ordo-liberals, we consider that the current avatar of capitalism, far from being directly deducible from the logic of capital, is only ever a historically specific 'economic-institutional figure', we must accept that the form of capitalism and crisis mechanisms are the contingent effects of certain legal rules, and not the necessary consequence of the laws of capitalist accumulation. Therewith they are open to being overcome through juridico-institutional changes,

---

7 Foucault, *Birth of Biopolitics*, p. 164.
8 Karl Marx and Frederick Engels, *Collected Works*, vol. 35, London: Lawrence & Wishart, 1996, p. 621 (*Capital*, vol. 1, Part Seven, Chapter XXV, section 2).

which fully justifies the legal interventionism demanded by neoliberalism. Once we are dealing with a specific capitalism, it becomes possible to intervene in it so as to create another capitalism, different from the first, which will itself represent a particular configuration determined by a set of juridico-political rules. Instead of an economic mode of production whose development is governed by a logic operating like some implacable 'natural law', capitalism is an 'economico-juridical complex' that can take a multiplicity of specific forms. This is also why we must refer to *neoliberal society*, not simply neoliberal *policy* or neoliberal *economics*. While undeniably a capitalist society, *this* society is a particular form of capitalism that needs to be analysed as such, in its irreducible specificity.

In some ways, Thomas Piketty's analysis in *Capital in the Twenty-First Century* resembles the Marxist account in its most mechanistic version, even though it has been subjected to the severest criticisms from Marxist economists. In it the marked rise in disparities of inheritance and income since the late twentieth century is essentially explained by the divergence between the growth rate of national income and the rate of returns on capital. Mechanically explicable, inexorable, spontaneous factors generate this long-term inegalitarian tendency. Periods of reduced inequalities are not attributable to social and ideological struggle, still less to political action, but to the 'exogenous shocks' represented by world wars and crises. Mechanics ultimately prevails over politics. Some passages are quite explicit: 'The return to a structurally high capital/income ratio in the twenty-first century, close to the levels observed in the eighteenth and nineteenth centuries, can therefore be explained by the return to a slow-growth regime.'[9] So the key factor is 'historical laws' that are largely independent of social and political relations. Public action is regarded as essentially reactive, never creative. As a result, the final part of the book, with its policy proposals (including a global tax), sits awkwardly with the whole preceding argument.[10] Thus, well may Piketty wish to 'supersede' Marx, but he shares with Marxist economists an unfortunate tendency to forget politics and its real effects on the economy and on social structures.[11]

To understand the crystallization of neoliberalism, we must above all avoid reducing the crisis of the 1960s and 70s to an 'economic crisis' in the traditional sense of the term. For neoliberalism responded not only to a crisis of *accumulation*, but also to a crisis of *governmentality*, which itself pertained to a severe crisis of hitherto dominant forms of power. Foucault's special merit was to situate the advent of a new way of conducting individuals in this context – a way that claimed to satisfy aspirations to freedom in every sphere, sexual and cultural as well as economic. Against economism, he grasped that the workers' struggles cannot be isolated from those of women, students,

9   Thomas Piketty, *Capital in the Twenty-First Century*, trans. Arthur Goldhammer, Cambridge, MA: Harvard University Press, 2014, p. 166.

10   For a converging critical commentary, see Nicolas Delalande, 'Vers une histoire politique du capital?', *Annales. Histoire, Sciences sociales*, vol. 70, no. 1, January–March 2015, pp. 47–59.

11   Unlike Paul Krugman, who stresses the decisive role of policies in the contrast between periods of convergence and divergence between income and inheritance. See *The Conscience of a Liberal: Reclaiming America from the Right*, London: Allen Lane, 2008.

artists or patients. He glimpsed the way in which the reorganization of methods of governing individuals in various social sectors, and reactions to social and cultural struggles, were assuming a coherence with neoliberalism that was at once theoretical and practical. His analysis was nevertheless limited in two respects, clearly identified by Wendy Brown when she refers to Foucault's 'relative indifference' to capital and democracy. On the one hand, he fails to take account of capitalism as a form of social domination; on the other, he does not analyse the effects of neoliberal rationality on democracy – its imaginary, principles, values and institutions.[12] No doubt this is a result of his choice of method. Focusing on governmental rationality, he aimed to explore new possibilities of ethical and political self-subjectivation in the spaces of freedom on which this rationality played.[13] If this limitation is to be remedied, by expanding the angle of reflection – that is, by trying to articulate neoliberal reason with the logic of capital – it can only be done by extending Foucault's examination of forms of governmentality.

In this regard, the key thing to understand is that in each of its previous phases the historical instantiation of capital has presupposed *symbolic formatting* and *institutional application*. In itself, at its highest level of abstraction, the logic of capital signifies nothing more

---

12 Brown, *Undoing the Demos*, pp. 73–8.
13 Strictly speaking, the question as to whether Foucault was neoliberal or anti-neoliberal is meaningless. It is often raised by those who seek to imprison him in a binary choice (of the type 'for or against the state' or 'for or against the market'), which was utterly foreign to him, as is well demonstrated by his remarks on 'state phobia' in his lecture of 7 March 1979 (*Birth of Biopolitics*, p. 187ff).

than 'production of surplus value'.[14] However, this logic does not represent some 'essence' of capitalism from which all social relations derive by dint of 'immanent' laws. Symbolic representation, repeated, coherent political interventions, and an abundant 'economico-juridical' output were indispensable in constructing this 'world of capital' or (as we have called it) the *becoming-global of capital*. The latter signifies that capital now knows no geographical bounds or separations between social spheres. A logic of *limitlessness* moves to impose itself in every domain.[15] Every individual is enjoined to become 'human capital'; every element of nature is regarded as a productive resource; every institution is considered an instrument of production. Natural and human reality is fully transcribed in the mathematical language of economics and management. This is the *imaginary* mainspring of neoliberalism, become self-evident, a necessity, reality itself. However, the metamorphosis of the world into capital no more pertains to an 'endogenous' law of economics than it does to some destiny of Western metaphysics. It is the historical result of a formidable mutation in the way of *governing* human beings and societies; it is the product of an institutional transformation whose potent social, subjective and environmental effects we are beginning to appreciate.

---

14   Marx and Engels, *Collected Works*, vol. 35, p. 614.

15   Jean-François Billeter speaks of a subjection of society to the 'law of the infinite', in the dual sense of an absence of any end-point and any goal (*Esquisses*, Paris: Éditions Allia, 2016, p. 82).

Extending the Boundaries of the Appropriation of Nature Ever Further

How is this logic of limitlessness imposed on nature? We inhabit a 'finite, completely known and occupied planet', and yet commodity logic can only live off its infinite expansion.[16] There are virtually no virgin spaces left; the fiction of *terra nullius*[17] is hard to mobilize, which rules out reproducing the logic of the 'New Frontier' that presided over the conquest of the West. As we have learnt from history, however, a frontier is posited by capital only to be crossed. And this occurs through the creation of norms and institutions. We can identify two novel forms of this implacable logic.

The prospect of the exhaustion of fossil fuels in the near future has prompted some states to encourage a veritable race to appropriate outer space. On 25 November 2015, a few days before the opening of COP21, Barack Obama signed a law – HR 2262 – authorizing such an appropriation, without undertaking a formal revision of the legal status of outer space.

Since the early 1960s, international law has cited 'the common interest of all mankind' in advocating the use of outer space for peaceful ends. The initial two articles of the 1967 space treaty fixed its legal status. The first recognized the right of every country to use outer space, implying

---

16 Sophie Bessis, *La double impasse. L'universel à l'épreuve des fondamentalismes religieux et marchands*, Paris: Éditions La Découverte, 2014, p. 18.

17 In Roman law, this term refers to a territory without an owner whose first occupier can appropriate it at will. It served to justify the colonization of America by the Europeans.

equal accessibility. The second stipulated that 'outer space, including the Moon and other celestial bodies, is not subject to national appropriation by claim of sovereignty, by means of use or occupation, or by any other means.' Both these aspects – usage open to all and non-appropriability – refer to the only subjects recognized in international law, namely, states: 'national appropriation' is appropriation by states, and non-appropriability is non-appropriability by states.

It is precisely this limit that the law signed on 25 November 2015 very adroitly exploits. Its name says it all: Competitiveness Act. In one of its provisions, it vests a US citizen engaged in commercial recovery of a resource located on an asteroid or in space with the right to own, possess, transport, use and sell the resource obtained in accordance with existing law. This amounts to granting US companies a formal property right, with all its exclusive, absolute character.[18] Yet the law adopted by Congress denies claiming direct territorial sovereignty over what will be open to being appropriated thus: the occupation and appropriation are not the deed of the USA as a state.[19] Thus we have an act of state sovereignty that circumvents the proscription of appropriation by state sovereignty without formally violating it. It involves a kind of 'delegation' whereby the state grants its citizens a legal title that it denies itself, the better to guarantee it to those to whom it has delegated it. But the loophole in the 1967 treaty is only asking to be expanded still further: what is not appropriable by states becomes

---

18   See the blog of S.I. Lex, 'Le jour où l'espace a cessé d'être un bien commun', 30 November 2015, scinfolex.com.
19   Ibid.

terra nullius for private companies. Thus the government of Luxemburg has created a structure equipped with a budget – SpaceResources.lu – intended to give private operators confidence in their right to appropriate the scarce minerals extracted from asteroids.[20]

A second form of the logic of limitlessness is to be found in the financialization of biodiversity. The marketization of nature is justified in the name of what must now be called 'biodiversity compensation'.[21] This does not mean that we do not have the right to destroy biodiversity, but that we have this right on condition of replacing what we have destroyed. For example, we have the right to destroy ten hectares of forest here so long as we plant ten hectares elsewhere, with the excuse that in thirty years' time, when the trees have grown, it will make no difference. However, to effect this compensation, the amount of the loss to be compensated must first be assessed. It is therefore necessary to assign a value to what is not a product of labour – for example, the pollination of trees and flowers by bees.

The notion of 'services' rendered by nature, susceptible to economic valuation, thus tends to become established. Biodiversity had hitherto been presented as a set of *resources* consisting in separate elements (genes, species, reserves, etc.) that could be possessed, bought and sold. In this classical form, marketization still involved the idea of the intrinsic value of biodiversity. Now we hear talk of

---

20   The declared goal of this initiative is 'to stimulate growth on Earth and open new horizons for the exploration of space': governement.lu, 2 February 2016.

21   Sandrine Feydel and Christophe Bonneuil, *Prédation. Nature, le nouvel Eldorado de la finance*, Paris: Éditions La Découverte, 2015, p. 67ff.

'ecosystemic services', consisting in flows from a stock of natural capital which, when combined with human industrial activities, creates human welfare.[22] Therewith the intrinsic value of biodiversity is erased in favour of the value attributed to the flows generated by natural capital, to the point where some do not shy away from the conclusion that the entire biosphere must be securitized as 'natural capital'. The significance of this alteration may be summarized thus: 'Inclusion of the biosphere in the market sphere does not simply take the form of *merchandise* (logic of the sale of wood and industrial capitalism, marketization of "biological resources" and gene patents, etc.), but also and especially *assets* (i.e. securities creating an entitlement to future income, in the financial logic of profit).'[23] In this transition from the commodification of nature to its financialization, a frontier has been extended which is no longer spatial: that of *valoriʒation*.

Limitlessness as a Regime of Subjectivity

The same logic of valorization is to be found at the very heart of neoliberal subjectivation. This is because such subjectivation is, in its way, a financial one. As a particular historical form of capitalism, neoliberalism comprises an essential imaginary dimension. Or rather, it is constituted and maintained solely by this dimension. Without it, it would be incapable of not merely surviving the gravest crises, but actually becoming fortified by them. Now, this

---

22   Ibid., pp. 59, 165.
23   Ibid., p. 166.

imaginary is basically an *entrepreneurial imaginary* and not a market imaginary. If we do not grasp this, we shall be condemned to impotence. Endlessly to bang on about the need to counter neoliberal policies with a Keynesian, redistributive economic policy is to fail to understand that neoliberalism can only be fought by opposing an *alternative imaginary* to its imaginary – an imaginary commensurate with the one it seeks to supplant in offering a desirable way of life. Nothing short of the power of an imaginary can create the desire to change the world. Allowing ourselves to be imprisoned in a discussion about the economic 'feasibility' of some particular proposal is to have lost the game in advance. For it is the neoliberal imaginary that compels people to situate themselves on this terrain. And since that imaginary is what gives neoliberalism its incomparable power, we need to examine whence its attraction, even to the worst-off, derives. In other words, what, in its content, makes it seem like the bearer of a promise of freedom within reach of every individual?

To assess the attraction and influence of neoliberalism, we must obviously decline to be taken in by the contemporary infatuation with training methods such as Cross Fit, modelled on US Navy exercises.[24] There is no doubt that such methods, which introduce the challenge and performance culture into the sphere of leisure activities by urging their adepts to continually 'surpass themselves', form part of the activity of neoliberal normativity. It is no less certain that they might satisfy the need for confidence on the part of stressed managers girding themselves to face a

---

24   See Pascale Krémer, 'Fais-moi mal, coach!', *Le Monde*, 14–15 June 2015, p. 19.

gamut of situations. And few will dispute that the fashion for a coach in 'personal branding', or self-marketing, is a further symptom of the neoliberalization of subjects. But such methods, even when combined with one another, even when widespread, do not create a social imaginary capable of accessing the internal self of every individual.

It is much better to turn to the model for people's lives represented by the corporation *in itself*. We then perceive a kind of co-extensiveness of life and corporation by dint of which the latter emerges less as a judicial construct than as a fully-fledged life-form. Such are the words of Marie-Vorgan Le Barzic, delegate general of NUMA (the association of innovative and start-up enterprises) on 10 November 2014, during the social entrepreneurship week organized by the newspaper *Libération*: 'Today, all citizens are taking control of their lives like a company' – before proceeding to correct herself: 'not yet all'.[25] In its very ingenuousness, the declaration is significant: each citizen's relationship to her life is analogous to the relationship between an entrepreneur and her business. Not that life itself is a business. Rather, one's conduct of life is analogous to the conduct of a business. Aside from the fact that the claim decks itself out in the best of intentions by constantly invoking the 'social', the most interesting thing is the stress on the notion of 'entrepreneurship'. Entrepreneurship goes far beyond the status of entrepreneur, which is necessarily limited to a minority of citizens. In fact, it constitutes a 'form of citizenship', portending a 'renewal of democracy'.[26]

---

25 At urlz.fr/36c5.
26 Ibid.

It would be wrong to assimilate this claim to the discourse of Nicolas Sarkozy or Christine Lagarde vaunting the merits of being a 'self-entrepreneur'. That involved diffusing the enterprise culture throughout society by encouraging a race to the bottom at the expense of skilled artisans. The praise of 'entrepreneurship' goes much further. Not only because the status of self-entrepreneur is still a legal one, but more fundamentally because, with entrepreneurship, the individual's *entire* existence is annexed by the logic of business, to the point of becoming the training ground for what should be called an 'entrepreneurial democracy'. 'Citizenship' itself is therefore no longer a matter of legal or political status. It is no longer a matter of rights and duties. It becomes conflated with each individual's management of her own existence. In this sense, 'entrepreneurial democracy' goes far beyond the political sphere proper. It is democracy placed, as it were, within easy reach – a non-delegable, non-representative democracy, since it is a matter of everyone's relationship to themselves, of the choice of oneself, and hence of autonomy and responsibility. Everyone becomes responsible for how they lead their life. This does not make everyone an 'entrepreneur', at least in the statutory sense of the term. But, it will be asked, how can someone who is not an entrepreneur conduct her life *like* an enterprise? If in order to be an 'entrepreneur' it is necessary *to own* an enterprise, to participate in 'entrepreneurship' it is sufficient *to be* an enterprise. The 'citizen' in 'entrepreneurial democracy' *is* herself an enterprise, so that this democracy is not so much that of the citizen-entrepreneur as that of the citizen-enterprise. This is why she runs her life 'in the manner' of an enterprise –

in the way she would run an enterprise if she had one. Here democracy consists in giving everyone the chance to conduct the enterprise they themselves are in whatever way they wish, making them wholly responsible for this conduct and its results, failures and successes alike.

To understand this decisive point, it is worth pausing over the theory of 'human capital' developed by American neo-liberalism.[27] Its originality consists in completely reversing the relationship between the subject and her work as conceived by a certain tradition of political economy in the wake of Marxism. Marx famously distinguished between labour and labour-power, and between labour-power and the person of the worker. Of these three concepts, labour-power is unquestionably the key one. The worker possesses a labour-power, composed of aptitudes and skills, which is nothing other than a commodity with a determinate value. In selling this commodity to the capitalist, the worker cedes the use of it for a specified duration in exchange for a wage. Labour, or the activity of labour, consists in an expenditure of labour-power for a quantitatively specified period of time. In this perspective, labour counts as 'abstract labour' – that is, labour rendered homogenous by what the market determines as socially necessary for the production of some particular commodity. In other words, the labourer *has* a labour-power, which she expends during the labour process; her main concern is the value at which she sells her

---

27   On this theory, developed by Theodor W. Schulz and Gary Becker, readers are referred to Michel Foucault's lecture of 14 March 1979 in the course on *The Birth of Biopolitics*. See also Luca Paltrinieri, 'Quantifier la qualité', *Raisons politiques*, no. 52, November 2013, pp. 88–108.

labour-power to the capitalist. The activity of labour itself is simply the application of this power in conditions decided by the capitalist.

The inversion operated by American neoliberals consists in adopting the standpoint of the subject who is in the process of working, or in regarding the worker as an 'active economic subject', dispensing altogether with the concept of labour-power. Labour will be broken down into capital and income: the worker's aptitude or skill will be regarded as a particular type of 'capital' and the wage as the 'income' of this capital. It will then be said that the worker derives a certain income from her skill-capital, or that this income is the product of, or return on, that capital. Any source of future income is a capital, but skill-capital differs significantly from other forms of capital – those invested in an enterprise by its proprietor. What is special about skill-capital is that it cannot be separated from the very person of the worker – hence its utter difference from labour-power. Whereas labour-power can be ceded or 'alienated' because it can be separated from the person of the labourer, skill-capital cannot be 'alienated' because it cannot be separated from the person of the labourer. It is not something ceded temporarily via a work contract, but coextensive with the whole life of the worker *qua* worker. It comprises both innate elements and acquired characteristics, primarily education and training. That is why it warrants being called 'human capital'. Labour-power is a *commodity* one possesses without being it, whereas skill is a *capital* which one does not possess but is. While people can always separate themselves from what they have, they can never separate themselves from what they are. The labourer is thus her own capital, since she is the source of her income. In this sense, she is an 'entrepreneur of herself'.[28]

The significance of this idea of enterprise, erected into a model for subjects of the relationship to the self, cannot be overstated. Everyone is a form of capital – a value to be ever more valorized throughout one's life, by means of investment. We know that money relates to itself in the mode of self-valorization (M-M' is the formula for financial capitalism).[29] It might be said that the subject who relates to herself in the manner of self-valorization (S-S') is the subject who has become financial capital for herself or financial capital made subject, capital itself as a form of subjectivation. And it is precisely in this sense that we may refer to neoliberal subjectivation as financial subjectivation. It may not be the promise of universal enrichment made by Plutus to the citizens of Athens in Aristophanes' comedy. But universal extension of the enterprise in the form of an unlimited multiplication of self-enterprises is a subjective spring that should not be ignored.

This is firstly because, despite everything, the big corporation as an institution still plays the role of model here, and it is therefore its logic which is, as it were, internalized by subjects, even though its gigantic size and character as a collective actor render it inaccessible to the individual subject. The self-enterprise has the subject internalize the logic of competition, especially via innovation, by making it her

---

28   Foucault, *Birth of Biopolitics*, p. 230 (translation modified).
29   Karl Marx and Frederick Engels, *Collected Works*, vol. 32 ('Theories of Surplus Value'), London: Lawrence & Wishart, 1989, p. 450ff.

duty to maximize her gains and thereby 'self-maximize'. None of this results from the operation of the spontaneous laws of capital accumulation. On the contrary, it is the outcome of power mechanisms constructed by targeting individuals.

Secondly, and consequently, on this new terrain the 'accumulation drive' finds material for self-development in a novel way. It has rightly been noted that big corporations opened up a new space for the tendency to unlimited accumulation, which assumed an anonymous and systemic character, by taking the separation between owner and manager already identified by Marx very much further.[30] Neoliberal financialization has made the corporation the maximizing institution par excellence, one whose logic is to some degree independent of the individual capitalist's desire for enrichment. At the same time, however, with financial subjectivation the 'accumulation drive' tends to be generalized to all individuals, opening up a new field for the operation of the tendency to limitlessness. For the limitlessness of accumulation is far from ruling out any form of pleasure. Against an idyllic view of the original capitalist as completely abstinent, Marx himself relativized the conflict

---

30 Stéphane Haber, 'Marx, Foucault et la grande entreprise comme institution centrale du capitalisme', in *Marx et Foucault. Lectures, usages, confrontations*, eds Christian Laval, Luca Paltrinieri and Ferhat Taylan, Paris: Éditions La Découverte, 2015, p. 313. It is in *Capital*, Volume Three, that Marx introduces the distinction between the ownership of capital and the role of director – a distinction that assumes increasing importance with the development of interest-bearing capital, the expansion of credit, and joint-stock companies. In today's terminology, ownership is embodied by the banker or shareholder, whereas the director's role is embodied by the manager.

between 'pleasure drive' and 'accumulation drive'. At a certain stage of development of his capital, the capitalist 'can ... live a more jolly life, and at the same time show more "abstinence"'.[31] But he extended the analysis by asserting that the industrial capitalist becomes more or less incapable of performing his role 'as soon as he wants the accumulation of pleasures instead of the pleasure of accumulation'.[32] We must attend to the rhetorical figure of chiasmus: it signifies that the enjoyment which makes capitalism wholly fit for its social purpose is not of the order of consumption; that enjoyment is not the end to which the accumulation of value aspires. The capitalist imperative is not 'accumulate *in order* to enjoy', or 'enjoy *while* accumulating', but 'enjoy accumulating' – that is, 'enjoy the production and expansion of value'.[33]

If we take the trouble to translate this injunction in terms of subjectivation, we obtain an identification of the subject with the expansion of her own value. Capitalist discourse, in its neoliberal form at any rate, does not so much dangle the promise of a saturation of desire through consumption as that of a plenitude achieved in unlimited expansion of the value which the subject represents for herself. Herein lies the truth of 'human capital': the value that is ever more valorized is no longer simply the means to enjoyment, it

---

31   Marx and Engels, *Collected Works*, vol. 35, p. 604 (*Capital*, Volume One, Chapter XXIV, section 4).

32   Karl Marx and Frederick Engels, *Collected Works*, vol. 31 ('Theories of Surplus Value'), London: Lawrence & Wishart, 1989, p. 180.

33   On this point, see Pierre Dardot, 'Du sujet divisé à la subjectivation capitaliste', *Critique*, nos 800–801, January–February 2014, p. 152.

becomes the *object* of enjoyment. The self-enhanced subject is one who enjoys the value that she is for herself.

In what sense should we take this promise of enjoyment? The term is to be understood in its Lacanian sense: enjoyment is not pleasure, which is still of the order of limits in that it is the satisfaction of a tendency, but beyond pleasure in that it is *self*-enjoyment exceeding any limit.[34] That is why it pertains to the impossible. How can the neoliberal condition be represented as attained and accomplished? Martin Crimp is the author of a remarkable play, *In the Republic of Happiness*, which may be regarded as a peerless dramatization of the imaginary of performance/enjoyment.[35] The closing third act is likewise entitled 'In the Republic of Happiness'. In fact, it is only now that we are truly *in* the Republic of Happiness. So says the character Uncle Bob, who clarifies the condition of citizens in this strange republic. Bob tells Madeleine that he does not remember what he said a moment ago and that he cannot recall how she is either. Along with memory, it is the world itself that is fading: 'the landscape is indistinct', 'the room is completely empty', there are no more 'citizens'. Loss of memory and loss of the world are the price to be paid for unlimited enjoyment: where plenitude in the relationship to self is supposed to prevail, there is no longer any alterity, either in oneself or outside oneself. The truth is that there is no 'good limitlessness'. There is a shared human condition only in the sense of limitation. The terrifying promise of the neoliberal

---

34 See Dardot and Laval, *The New Way of the World*, p. 296ff.
35 Martin Crimp, *In the Republic of Happiness*, London: Faber & Faber, 2012.

Plutus is a happiness impossible to share. The 'Republic of Happiness' is the impossibility of self-enjoyment, and the limitlessness of self-enjoyment is the graveyard of political democracy.

4

The European Union, or, The Empire of Norms

Members of the European Union cannot invoke popular sovereignty to oppose rules whose constitutional value trumps the general will of citizens: 'There can be no democratic choice against the European treaties.'[1] The European institutions, Commission and Council combined, even grant themselves the right to scheme against a democratically elected government, to support the opposition to it, and to destabilize an entire economy to effect its overthrow, as we saw after Syriza's electoral victory in late January 2015. In this sense, the 'Greek lesson' is of the utmost significance for appreciating how things really stand with the 'European project'. Having finally emerged from the period of approximations and experimentation, the semi-silence of 'liberals' and the smoke-screens of 'social democrats', Europe has entered a new phase – as a new power which reveals and proclaims itself such, functioning as an empire

---

1   Jean-Claude Juncker, *Le Figaro*, 29 January 2015.

of an unprecedented kind, founded on the inflation of legal and economic norms.

The 'European Project': From the Narrative of Origins to Historical Reality

Why does the 'continent of fundamental freedoms' today seem like an 'iron cage of the peoples of Europe', to adopt Yanis Varoufakis's excellent formula? To answer this question, we must extricate ourselves from the justification of the 'European project', which still functions as an incontestable ideal. The narrative of origins tells a beautiful tale. For years, nationalist passions and totalitarian ideologies resulted in Europeans savagely massacring one another. But the happy creation of a 'European community', based on people's clearly understood interests, has made it possible to avert any new devastating wars. This narrative, which embellishes the role of the 'founding fathers' – depicting them as so many latter-day Lycurguses – has always functioned as a promise: uniting the 'friends of freedom' against totalitarianism in all its guises, only the 'European project' can protect the peoples of the continent from another internecine war. Such is the basis of the shared belief that has enabled the consolidation of what would be a new empire of peace and prosperity, underwritten by the progressive codification of a *jus publicum economicum europaeum* – a new *jus commune* aspiring to supersede the Roman law of the Empire or the canon law of the mediaeval Church. We can see why this fine project was so appealing. In any event, it has operated as a supreme legitimizing principle. The final goal has justified everything – every renunciation, every delegation, every capitulation, all the blackmail and all the slippages which, from text to text, directive to directive, legal decision to legal decision, have authorized regulatory and legislative control over the life of Europe's peoples by unelected structures. The grimly prosaic reality now forces itself on us: it has only been possible to construct this happy empire, which aimed to turn the page on totalitarianism, *behind the people's back*, by slow but sure dispossession of the springs of popular sovereignty.

Everything, or almost, has been commandeered to lend historical legitimation to this edifying narrative. Anxious to identify an ancestor, the European Union found one in Charlemagne's Frankish empire, rather than in a Roman Empire unduly centred on the southern and eastern shores of the Mediterranean. As Bryan Ward-Perkins observes: 'The centre of the present-day European Union, the Strasbourg–Frankfurt–Brussels triangle, and the centre of the eighth- and ninth-century Frankish empire coincide very closely: Brussels, for instance, is little more than 100 kilometres from Charlemagne's favoured residence and burial place at Aachen.'[2] No matter that Charlemagne forced the Lombards to hand over the kingdom of Italy, and ordered the massacre of thousands of Saxons: the only thing that counts is the image of the builder of a post-Roman empire dominated by the Franks. What is more, the Franks can be portrayed as ancestors of the French and Germans alike. Thus, in 1965 a major exhibition in Aachen presented

---

2 Bryan Ward-Perkins, *The Fall of Rome and the End of Civilization*, Oxford: Oxford University Press, 2006, p. 175.

Charlemagne as 'the first emperor who sought to unite Europe'. In 1996, a second major exhibition commemorated the 1500th anniversary of the baptism of Clovis under the title 'The Franks, Precursors (or Pathfinders) of Europe'.[3] Once again, the image of 'the powerful Germanic warrior accepted into the Catholic faith by the Gallo-Roman bishop of Reims' was too tempting for historical reality not to be sacrificed to utterly anachronistic mythology – that of a 'Franco-German' core of the Carolingian Empire!

To expose the mystificatory dimensions of this self-legitimation in full, we must first consider the way that the 'European question' appears to anyone who undertakes to examine the historical reality over the *longue durée*. To this end, let us consult the indications provided by Michel Foucault in his course on *The Birth of Biopolitics* in 1978–79, notwithstanding their often allusive character. In his lecture of 24 January 1979 at the Collège de France,[4] Foucault sought to distil the 'new idea of Europe' that emerged in the mid-eighteenth century with the classical liberalism not only of Adam Smith, but also of Kant. This Europe was neither the imperial, Carolingian Europe inheriting the Roman Empire, nor the Europe of the balance of power consecrated by the Treaty of Westphalia in 1648. It was a 'collective economic subject' which, in and through competition between states, paved the way for 'unlimited economic progress'. In the Europe of classical liberalism, *competition* between states replaced *balance* of power.[5] Europe made

---

3   Ibid.
4   Foucault, *Birth of Biopolitics*, p. 51ff.
5   Michel Foucault, *Security, Territory, Population: Lectures at the Collège*

such competition the guarantee of 'collective enrichment', which meant that the issue of peace was now posed very differently. Whereas in the seventeenth century, states' mutual limitation appeared as the foundation of 'perpetual peace', in the eighteenth century it was the unlimited character of the external market, or 'commercial globalization', that seemed to guarantee peace. By virtue of its boundlessness, commercial competition between states was perceived as a guarantee of collective prosperity and, consequently, as a factor in maintaining peace.

But, it will be asked, what is the relationship between this *liberal* Europe and the *neoliberal* Europe constructed in the aftermath of the Second World War? Ever since its foundation, the European Union has claimed to be the heir of liberal Europe in adopting the objective of perpetual peace *through* market competition. The insistent reference to the Kantian project might create the impression of continuity in this filiation: perpetual peace as the goal, the market as the means to prosperity, and prosperity as the guarantee of peace. However, what has changed profoundly is both the whole character of this market and its relationship to states and political institutions. The market to be constructed is first and foremost the *European* market itself, and competition between states is not so much a means as the very principle of the construct that will guarantee peace.

For a better understanding, we must take a detour via the history of post-war Germany. If 1945 was perhaps not 'Germany, year zero', it certainly was 'German state, year

de France 1977–78, ed. Michel Senellart, trans. Graham Burchell, Houndmills and New York: Palgrave Macmillan, 2007, pp. 300–1.

zero'. The ordo-liberals made a successful market economy the legitimizing principle of the state to be reconstructed.[6] Keeping things in proportion, the principle of the market economy was likewise charged, from the start, with legitimizing the whole European construct. Obviously, to this day there is no European state, but European political institutions exist that have been legitimized by the same principle. No covert German strategy is to be found here, seeking to make up for Germany's political and military inferiority by economic hegemony. This is not a re-edition of the negotiation of the Treaty of Westphalia: the Europe of the Treaty of Rome is not a new 'way of making Germany forget the Empire',[7] still less a way of turning Europe into a German empire. Instead, it involves a trajectory which, from minor regulatory step to major constitutional step, ultimately discloses its overall coherence. What long seemed to be a random set of processes, a mosaic of dispersed efforts, has over time and through various ordeals ended up close to the image of coherence that pro-Europeans always wished for. The history of the European project has developed in line with opportunities and obstacles, with moments of acceleration and extensions that had not been programmed, but in a very precisely determined direction.[8]

---

6   Foucault, *Birth of Biopolitics*, p. 81ff.

7   Foucault, *Security, Territory, Population*, p. 304.

8   We have highlighted the logic governing the construction of Europe in *The New Way of the World*, Chapters 3 ('Ordo-Liberalism between "Economic Policy" and "Policy of Society"') and 7 ('The Ordo-Liberal Origins of the Construction of Europe'). Readers are also referred to Chapter 2 above.

The Construction of the Mega Market

On close, sober examination, the 'European project' turns out to be the *process* of construction of a market gradually endowed with its own operational rules and its own institutional apparatus, charged with extending, maintaining and strengthening it. With its bodies, jurisprudence and civil servants, the European Union is first and foremost the economic and legal operator of this construction. Building a competitive market requires subjecting society to the exigencies of competitiveness through the kind of interventionism elaborated and advocated by ordo-liberalism. For the latter the point is to intervene in the market's conditions of existence through 'coordinating actions' – what, in ordo-liberal terminology, is called a 'framework policy'. In this regard, Foucault mentions that in 1952 Walter Eucken recommended intervening in a number of areas (population, technology, education, legal regime of agriculture, availability of soil, climate, etc.) to integrate European agriculture into the market economy. He observes that Eucken's prescriptions in many ways anticipated the 'Common Agricultural Market of the next decade' and even the 1968 Mansholt Plan, with its programme to restructure community agriculture.[9]

This is how the ordo-liberal road map for constructing a 'market order', or 'competitive order', determined the direction of Europe's construction from the outset, even if this orientation was only accomplished much later, in accordance with the balance of forces in Europe and a

---

9   Foucault, *Birth of Biopolitics*, p. 141.

much more auspicious global context. The initial agreement, which has never been challenged, was as follows: the 'European Community' was to be organized as a regulated market not by social rules or moral principles, but by *rules of competition*, and bounded by a stable currency framework, the whole being guaranteed by bodies independent of national politics. As we have seen,[10] ordo-liberals were responsible for the crucial idea that the basic rule of the European 'economic constitution' is *free, undistorted competition* – a formula already found in the 1957 Treaty of Rome. It is the fundamental, core principle of the European Community's, and then the European Union's, economic law and political order. The key point is that the market pertains to a 'constitutional decision' which is the foundation of the *Rechtsstaat* and 'social market economy'. The jurist Josef Drexl put it quite explicitly: 'The founding states took a constitutional decision of the greatest importance in favour of the competitive order'[11] – a decision confirmed, extended and crystallized in every judgement of the European Court of Justice, not to mention the incessant activity of the European Commission to that end. Drexl sums up what the French, far from alone in their deafness, have never wished to hear: 'The ordo-liberals, who dominated economic policy in post-war Germany, had a decisive influence on the content of the Treaty of Rome and the European Economic Community.'[12]

---

10 See Chapter 2 above.

11 Josef Drexl, 'La constitution économique européenne. L'actualité du modèle ordolibéral', *Revue internationale de droit économique*, no. 4, 2011, p. 438.

12 Ibid.

However disagreeable, the truth is that Europe is today *more openly ordo-liberal than Germany itself*, at least constitutionally.[13] Repeating the work of their distant, state-building mediaeval ancestors, for seven decades Europe's legists – jurists, economists, experts and civil servants or simply politicians – have endeavoured to construct markets and reorganize societies on this doctrinal basis. The first 'market-makers' strove to perfect a veritable *machine for manufacturing norms* which, progressively creating the European mega market, has ended up working by itself, via directives, judgements, regulations and treaties. This represents the roll-out of a normative logic, embodied by an administrative apparatus specifically dedicated to it, which has gradually imposed the 'basic provisions' of competition, according to the prevailing formula in the European Court of Justice's body of jurisprudence.

This (let us repeat) is not some Germanic peculiarity and still less a kind of 'German essence', as a prevalent but unacceptable Germanophobia would have it. The 'European project' could not have been initiated and pursued without the consent and active participation of other European, notably French, leaders. Agreement on the 'institutional market', in the words of Jacques Rueff, a vanguard neoliberal economist and subsequently a judge in the Court of Justice of the European Community, made it possible to unify multiple currents and numerous political leaders.

---

13   We therefore maintain that Hayek's influence on the construction of Europe has been exaggerated. Wolfgang Streeck goes so far as to refer to a '*Hayekization* of European capitalism', the better to enjoin a restoration of national sovereignty (*Buying Time*, p. 103).

The French metanarrative of the 'modernization' sought
by Europe's 'founding fathers' is nothing but a myth
designed to conceal the underlying logic of the construction of Europe. A significant proportion of France's élites
considered the national parliamentary system to be archaic,
ineffective, and even dangerous at a time when Communist
parties were still powerful in several countries. Jean Monnet,
Robert Schuman and those who with them formed the clan
of 'modernizers' in post-war France aimed to circumvent
parliamentarism.[14] The very term 'Community' is a lure
that embellishes the reality. Monnet and Schuman sought
above all to promote regulation of a common market by an
authority independent of political parties, deemed inherently
dangerous because ideological.[15] Convergence on the idea
of independence for the authorities responsible for markets
regulation was variously justified, and the Franco–German
alliance was forged from different perspectives. Already
in 1930s France, there was a planning and modernizing
project advanced by (among others) partisans of an anti-
parliamentary 'third way' and supported by experts who
believed in a strong state independent of political parties.
Some of them, who later reappeared in the company of the
'founding fathers', had in the interim sympathized with the
communitarian ideology of Vichy's National Revolution, if
not with the Nazi *Volksgemeinschaft*. Whether we like it or
not, the planners in post-war France were not all congenial,
redistributive Keynesians. Their faith in the virtues of free

---

14   See Antonin Cohen, *De Vichy à la Communauté européenne*, Paris:
Presses Universitaires de France, 2012.

15   Ibid., p. 64.

trade supervised by a supranational power made them see in the 'European Community' a chance to apply their hostility to 'politicking', along with their technocratic desire to prevent the irrational meddling of citizens in the smooth administration of things.

From the late 1980s, with communism having disappeared from the landscape and parliamentary government increasingly subordinate to the executive, the development of the European mega market formed part of a strategy for circumventing and undermining social resistance to national neoliberal policies. The Commission drew on the 'strategic resources of the market' to reinforce its own positions.[16] But what is true of the Commission is true of all the economico-political elites, who regarded completion of the mega market, and then monetary union, as the way to press home their political and social advantage. Presented as a way of accelerating the 'modernization' of societies, by aligning them with the new global order, the 'market strategy' underpinned the reinforcement of the power of European institutions. But, at the same time, it enabled holders of economic and political power nationally to increase their own power over wage-earners and over the ruled as a whole. Two birds with one stone, so to speak. The strategy was neither linear nor simple; and it was not always coherent. There were many obstacles and inevitable tensions, because since the mid-twentieth century, and even the late nineteenth in some cases, national states had embarked on a different and, in many respects, contrary course: the construction of

---

16 See Nicolas Jabko, *L'Europe par le marché. Histoire d'une stratégie improbable*, Paris: Les Presses de Sciences Po, 2009.

forms of social protection and public services. The objective of the 'market-makers' has always been to intensify competition not only between states, but within each state. To stand any chance of success, this cannot be done country by country, but only through a supranational strategy of normative diktat aimed at creating an irreversible situation, inaccessible to national citizens. This path accounts for the 'success' of European construction: constructing, over and above national spaces, an institutional market system that is incumbent on all countries, and which allows economic and political elites to steer clear of the 'dirty work' of contesting established 'social rights'.

We need to assess the significance of opting for European integration through competition, rather than political cooperation or social solidarity. Here we have a point of rupture with Europe's political past that cannot be stressed enough. A vast coalition of Right and Left has formed around a 'European project' that aims to replace the old relations of domination and adversity between European countries by competition – and this happened at the very moment when competition was being imposed as the new global norm. Such 'ideological coagulation' was the prelude to the well-nigh incontestable domination of the ordo-liberal schema of market regulation. With the Single European Act of 1986 and the Maastricht Treaty of 1992, there was no going back.

The 'Expertocratic' Governance of the European Union

In order to play down the role of the European Union, some of its zealots argue that 32,000 civil servants are no match for the power of national civil services; that the European budget is derisory; that the EU has neither army, nor any real diplomatic corps, nor even an exciting 'narrative'. All this is true. However, if we stop there, we shall miss the key thing: the European Union functions as an *empire of law* and it is this normative output that accounts for its formidable power. The European Union is not a federal state, or an 'international super-state' or 'supranational Leviathan'.[17] It is a system of government based on the rule of law, which is itself to be aligned with the supreme logic of the market. The 'mixed mechanism' of governance[18] (a pseudo-federal form for the Commission, a confederal form for the Council) prioritizes inter-state accords without this representing an obstacle to the system's overall operation, since the latter essentially functions in accordance with market norms.

This system did not spring from the brain of some neoliberal theoretician. Practice often preceded norms and laws. No decision-making centre planned the various stages of the construct. European institutions developed in 'perpetual motion',[19] or more exactly in a process of self-construction. The EU forged itself through law.[20] To construct the market is to generate norms. For the oligarchies soldered together by their attachment to the 'European project', to

---

17   According to Streeck's formulae in *Buying Time*, p. 114, and 'Small-State Nostalgia? The Currency Union, Germany and Europe: A Reply to Jürgen Habermas', *Constellations*, vol. 21, no. 2, 2014, p. 219.

18   A term borrowed from Étienne Balibar, 'Europe et réfugiés: l'élargissement', 15 September 2015, Mediapart.

19   Antonin Cohen, *Le Régime politique de l'Union européenne*, Paris: La Découverte, 2014, p. 7.

20   Antoine Vauchez, *L'Union par le droit. L'invention d'un programme institutionnel pour l'Europe*, Paris: Les Presses de Sciences Po, 2013.

construct the market is therefore also to *construct themselves* as a source of generation of norms – the opposite of some continuous emanation from a strategic centre, generating each decision out of a long-term vision. 'Brussels bureaucracy', 'Eurocracy' and 'expertocracy' are simply formulae for referring to this apparatus of normative output and its agents. People are sometimes surprised by the inflexibility of the rules. But the strict observance of norms has always been posited as an absolute precondition for the 'common market': hence the need to create a court, judges, barristers and sanctions, to confer the aspect of an iron corset, a punitive character, on Europe.

What in bureaucratic jargon is habitually called the *acquis communautaire* is a pile of tens of thousands of norms imposed on national laws – among them the twenty European treaties and thousands of 'legislative acts', not to mention recommendations and opinions. This is an opaque universe populated by unreadable texts, including the famous Lisbon Treaty that turned European 'citizenship' into a bad joke by reducing it, at best, to an appendix of citizenship of a nation-state;[21] and norms which have gone on accumulating and ramifying, far beyond the exclusive competences of the Union or even those shared between the EU and member-states. Thus, on the grounds of 'support and coordination competences', every domain of social existence has been 'captured' by European normativity –

---

21   Let us recall that the transitional measures adopted between 2003 and 2005 created inequality between 'European citizens' by suspending the right to circulation of wage-earning workers from the ten new member-states from the former Soviet bloc (see Teresa Pullano, *La Citoyenneté européenne. Un espace quasi étatique*, Paris: Les Presses de Sciences Po, pp. 111–39).

employment, tourism, culture, health and education.[22] And this normative output is self-inflating, if only because of the thousands of violations it prompts and the jurisprudential decisions resulting from referral of cases to the Court of Justice.

Since the start of the 2000s, this normative power, which is largely independent of national political authorities and, a fortiori, outside the control of ordinary citizens, has been known as 'European governance'.[23] The term 'governance' has, of course, the advantage of evoking the logic of consensus between non-state actors, more fluid and flexible than that informing the acts of a 'government' – a logic thought to favour centralization and hierarchy. It is a process of decision-making that conveniently avoids any formalization. If we transpose this method to the field of politics, we arrive at decision-making severed from any public deliberation on substantive issues and treated as a mere technical arrangement between already informed actors. 'Governance' reduces public life to *management* or administration by eliminating politics, conflict and deliberation over common values or ends.[24] As was clearly demonstrated by the Eurogroup's decision-making process in the case of Greece, opacity is the rule even when the fate

---

22   See Isabelle Bruno, Pierre Clément and Christian Laval, *La Grande mutation. Néolibéralisme et éducation en Europe*, Paris: Syllepse, 2010, and Sandrine Garcia, 'L'Europe du savoir contre l'Europe des banques? La construction de l'espace européen de l'enseignement supérieur', *Actes de la recherche en sciences sociales*, nos 166–167, March 2007, pp. 80–93.

23   See European Commission, *European Governance: A White Paper*, 2001.

24   See Brown, *Undoing the Demos*, pp. 127–8.

of a country and its people is at stake.[25] Appearances not-withstanding, we are at the antipodes of the 'administrative or industrial regime' dear to Saint-Simon. For the agents of governance are technicians and experts, not scientists. It is not so much the mastery of a *science* that qualifies and recommends them as the quality of their *experience*, which enables them to move from heading a bank to heading a government, or from the post of European commissioner to that of governor of the central bank.[26] Governance by experts is the ideal formula for the *denial of politics prac-ticed by politicians*. That is why it very precisely defines 'European governance'.

Even if it possesses its own logic, this apparatus of 'governance' is a creature of states. They equip it with nor-mative sovereignty to perform a task they would often find very difficult at the national level. Hence the importance of the 'independence' of European institutions from national authorities. This should not be regarded as a 'defect' or 'deficit', but as a crucial functional asset for realizing the great work of ordo-liberalism. The national state is directly subject to clashes between social forces and political groups. A supranational authority is better placed to escape these power relations and the impure compromises they force.

---

25 During a debate with the editors of Mediapart ('Face à la rédaction de Mediapart', 25 September 2015, YouTube, minutes 28–35), Yanis Varoufakis revealed that the Eurogroup met behind closed doors for ten hours without anyone taking notes. There are no minutes to which reference can be made to establish the positions adopted by the various participants. Such a modus operandi is revealing of the opacity of the practices of European governance.

26 Emblematic in this respect are the figures of Monti and Draghi, much more so than the convenient bogeyman of Wolfgang Schäuble as an ordo-liberal true believer.

That is why the assertion early on of the primacy of EU law over national law, and the prohibition on states opposing an act of the Community, even if it violates basic rights, were essential.[27] In fact, the national elites ultimately found their niche. Expertocratic governance makes the normative logic specific to 'independent' institutions dovetail with the combined interests of national economic and political elites. Thus, far from being incompatible with the inexorable power of the iron system that has prevailed for several decades, the flexible procedures of 'governance' actively help to produce and maintain that power.

Budget and Currency as Disciplinary Tools

The power of law is increasingly explicitly aligned with the absolute, unchecked legitimacy of capital accumulation and generalized competition. If we follow examinations of the internal balance within European institutions, we find the 'economic' core of governance has been considerably strengthened since the introduction of the euro and, even more so, since the 'crisis of the euro' in 2008–09. This core combines central bankers, members of the economic and financial directorate of the European Commission, finance ministers (particularly those of the eurozone) and senior civil servants at national finance and economics ministries.

---

27   In a judgement of 17 December 1970 (Internationale Handels-gesellschaft, 11/70, Rec. p. 1125), the Court of Justice ruled that 'the invocation of breaches either of basic rights as formulated in the Constitution of a member-state, or of the principles of a national constitutional structure, would not affect the validity of an act of the Community or its effect on the territory of that state'.

Educated at the same universities, these people, who have often worked in US investment banks, the OECD or the World Bank, form an 'integrated transnational ruling group under American domination', in the words of Frédéric Lebaron. Relying on constitutionalized economic rules, this group strives to 'supervise' national policies not only in the fiscal domain, but across the whole spectrum of government.[28] Hence the numerical rules fixed at Maastricht. They are easy to mock: as a proportion of GDP, the 3 per cent budget deficit or 60 per cent government debt refer to no macro-economic reality and have no historical precedent. In Europe, however, a figure is no mere statistical fabrication, but immediately valid as a norm, an absolute limit, a disciplinary tool. Once prescribed, the rule must be observed whatever the cost, even when it clashes with the best macroeconomic analysis and its effects are disastrous.

It was in the emergency context of 2010–12 that normative constraints were made harsher still, under the rubric of the 'new European economic governance'.[29] We have seen that the 'subprime' mortgage crisis triggered a sovereign debt crisis from late 2009. The financial crisis led to an increase in government debt in numerous member-states and to speculation on debt securities. This created a marked divergence in long-term interest rates between eurozone countries. Political and institutional responses to the crisis exposed growing tensions between groups of countries.

---

28   Frédéric Lebaron, 'Les dirigeants de la BCE, une nouvelle "élite" monétaire européenne?', in *Le champ de l'eurocratie. Une sociologie politique du personnel de l'UE*, ed. Didier Georgakakis, Paris: Economica, 2012, p. 124.

29   See Christophe Degryse, 'La nouvelle gouvernance économique européenne', *Courrier hebdomadaire du CRISP*, 2012.

Mutual distrust necessitated the strengthening of controls over national statistics, the creation of supreme budgetary bodies independent of political institutions, and, above all, the establishment of a whole series of controls and locks in the 2012 Treaty on Stability, Coordination and Governance (TSCG) and the subsequent directives and regulations that complemented it. European leaders thought they could gradually resolve the problem of government debt over twenty years by constitutionalizing a fiscal 'golden rule'. The idea behind these innovations was a priori monitoring of any national policy that might impact upon the budget, debt, employment or growth. Before national parliaments pronounce, economic and social orientations are subject to *ex ante* validation by the Commission, so that the monitoring system has become steering of a technocratic kind.[30] The slightest deviation from the norms is subject to warnings, involving the revision of plans and the threat of financial penalties.

The significance of the adoption of the Bundesbank model when creating the independent European Central Bank, on the basis of the 1989 Delors Report, cannot be exaggerated. Central bank independence having been elevated into a dogma by Walter Eucken's school, we may reckon that it marks the acme of ordo-liberal influence. That the ECB's mandate is to ensure the rigidity of monetary norms clearly illustrates how the construction of Europe has deliberately removed monetary issues from the

---

30   Corinne Gobin, 'L'Union européenne et la nouvelle gouvernance économique: un système politique contre l'État démocratique', *Pyramides*, no. 25, 2013, pp. 155–80.

public sphere of discussion and decision.[31] By conferring on this invisible, intangible institution absolute sovereignty in setting its key interest rates exclusively in line with its mission of currency stability, Europe has created a situation where money is no longer an instrument governed by political decisions. But this strict monetarism is not all. The independence of the ECB and especially the creation of the single currency, decided in 1992, have generated tools of economic and social discipline that are so many levers in the neoliberal homogenization of societies. Unable to resort to devaluation of national currencies, governments have had nowhere to turn but 'internal devaluation' in the form of slashed wages and social protections.

But the struggle for 'competitiveness' has not yielded the projected harmonization. German policy since 2002 has aggravated imbalances, divergences and instabilities, to the point of threatening the eurozone and European integration itself. The euro's path has proved to be full of perils and unintended consequences, as we have seen since 2010 in particular. Obviously, monetary integration is not the cause of all ills and neoliberal logic was in place prior to the euro. But its creation has unquestionably accentuated the operation of competitive mechanisms and increased the influence of fiscal and monetary discipline at the expense of any shared social objectives. The 'crisis of the euro' has made it possible to add on to the existing structure a set of

---

31   According to Article 105 of the Maastricht Treaty, the ECB's sole duty is to 'maintain monetary stability'. We see how far the illustrious precedent of the Bundesbank has been a model for the central banks of other European countries and then for the ECB itself (Streeck, *Buying Time*, pp. 32–3, n. 59).

institutional devices that impose similar austerity measures universally. If we consider the influence of the various institutions, it is the ECB that has most reinforced its power since 2010 – intervening in every episode of the euro crisis, in the forefront of the Greek crisis and taking a very tough position on fiscal rigour and structural reform. No doubt it has been compelled to pursue 'unconventional' monetary policies, lowering interest rates and buying government debt to reflate the economy. The purchase of sovereign debt, contravening the German governors' monetarist dogma, was dictated by fears of a collapse in growth. But to make this policy of 'quantitative easing' acceptable the ECB has significantly extended its sway, radicalizing its injunctions on fiscal matters and labour market reform.[32]

In What Way Is the European Union 'Social'?

A neoliberal proscription has long branded as illegitimate any question of 'social justice' in the European Union. And if the 'social question' is now at the heart of European economic construction, it is exclusively in terms of *competitiveness*. Far from leaving the 'social' to national politics, as they are often criticized for doing, the European Commission, the European Court of Justice and the ECB have become veritable organs of government of society, working to introduce greater 'flexibility' into the labour

---

32   Cf. Mario Draghi's very clear view making labour market reform a key objective for the ECB: 'Structural reforms, inflation and monetary policy', introductory speech by Mario Draghi, president of the ECB, ECB Forum on Central Banking, Sintra, 22 May 2015: urlz.fr/37Z0.

market so as to improve the overall performance of economic factors and raise Europe's 'growth potential', in accordance with official rhetoric.[33] Direct competition between 'posted workers', or indirect competition via different wage and social protection levels, constitute a formidable machine for eroding employment law and undermining what remains of the organized wage-earning class.[34] Not only does Europe fail to protect established social rights, it is actually destroying them. The now notorious decisions of the Court of Justice afford ample proof: its rulings between 2007 and 2008 represent a veritable 'revolution', finding every time for the freedom to produce services and goods and to start up enterprises, in the face of national employment law and collective agreements.[35]

Zealously constructing the market and then the single currency, the French and European 'Left' has actively worked to build a normative system that impedes any left-wing policy and ultimately entails the Left's own disappearance, to the benefit of the hard Right, xenophobia and nationalism. It is precisely *in and through Europe* that the self-destruction of social-democracy has accelerated, not only because the Left in the Party of European Socialists (PES) invariably votes in the European Parliament like the Right in the European People's Party (EPP), but above all

---

33   Commission of the European Communities, *Modernising Labour Law to Meet the Challenges of the Twenty-First Century*, Green Paper, 2006.

34   Recent reforms in Spain, Italy and France are a perfect illustration of this.

35   See Antoine Vauchez, *Démocratiser l'Europe*, Paris: Éditions du Seuil, 2014, pp. 70–1 and Alain Supiot, 'Le sommeil dogmatique européen', *Revue française des affaires sociales*, no. 1, 2012, pp. 185–98.

because European integration via competition has become the *actual content* of the national policies pursued by the 'Left'.

Even on the critical Left or among alter-globalists, Europe long remained an ill-defined entity, an unidentified political object. Its history, like its character, was not well-known. There was a desire to 'democratize Europe', to create a 'social Europe', following or alongside 'market Europe'. In a word, the 'left of the left' had not abandoned the idea of *inflecting* or *reorienting* the European Union in a more social, more democratic direction – and this despite the increasingly open rallying of 'social democrats' to the ordo-liberal project. Ignorance of the underlying logic of European construction derived from *national constriction* of the horizon of left-wing forces in Europe, which had become *essentially* uninterested in their European and international environment. The debate on the Constitutional Treaty in 2005 altered the picture by starkly revealing that, if actually existing Europe was decidedly 'social', it was not at all in the sense people had believed or hoped.

In reality, democratization is the last illusion of defenders of the 'European project'. Like social Europe, democratic Europe will not happen,[36] not in the current framework at any rate. For at stake are the very foundations of Europe, not some 'deficit' that could be remedied by an institutional supplement. That is why Yanis Varoufakis's 'Manifesto for Democratizing Europe' is doomed to failure. Not because it opens up the prospect of a European Constituent Assembly,

---

36   François Denord and Antoine Schwartz, *L'Europe sociale n'aura pas lieu*, Paris: Raisons d'agir, 2009.

but on account of the means it advocates. It calls in the immediate present for a democratization of the 'bureaucracy of the European Union' and imagines it can respond in the next twelve months to the current economic crisis 'with the help of current institutions and in the framework of existing treaties', through a 'creative reinterpretation' of them.[37] In reality, any initiative to democratize European institutions on existing constitutional bases is bound to turn its back on democracy. The Greek lesson is incontrovertible: in order to re-found Europe, it is necessary to break with the *whole* treaty system. The alternative is not 'nationalist regression or sticking with Europe', because the latter is precisely what is fuelling and exacerbating nationalism in its most abject forms. Europe can only be re-founded from below, by a transnational democratic citizenship that cannot be the work of anyone but European citizens themselves.

---

37   See Ludovic Lamant, 'L'Europe que dessine Yanis Varoufakis', 3 February 2016, Mediapart.

5
The Debt Noose

The Greek case is particularly revealing about 'neoliberal radicalization'. Here we have a country which, on 25 January 2015, elected a parliament whose majority was intent on ending the austerity policies that had over five years reduced the amount of wealth produced by one-quarter, pushed people into poverty, and raised the mortality rate. For six months, supposedly 'apolitical' European institutions – in close coordination with Greek oligarchs, the principal owners of the media – waged a veritable economic and ideological war on the Syriza government. Following a series of concessions that began in February, they brought it to the point of complete submission to the logic of austerity contained in the 'memorandums' signed since 2010 by Greek governments and the Troika (European Commission, ECB, IMF). Surrender was finally secured in July 2015, with the signature of the third memorandum approved on 19 August.[1]

---

1 For a chronology of the events with commentary, see Stathis

Debt as a Government Tool

It has been amply demonstrated that the euro, by its very modus operandi, has resulted in growing imbalances between the economies of the member-states while causing credit bubbles in Southern European countries, especially Spain and Greece. But this malfunctioning is not simply due to some technical design fault, as Paul Krugman imagines. It stems both from the economic balance of forces between countries and from the political conception of a currency developed by ordo-liberalism. In fact, the euro was introduced not as a monetary tool in the service of democratically determined policies, but as an inviolable element in the institutional and regulatory framework in which policy *absolutely must* be inscribed. The ordo-liberal conception of the currency is thus strictly disciplinary.[2] But how is this discipline exercised in the European Union? This is what we have learnt from the political war conducted by the European institutions against the government of the Greek radical Left in 2015. The direct blackmail used to get the Tsipras government to capitulate was the threat of expulsion from the eurozone, soon made concrete by the progressive monetary blockade by the ECB from the start of February. But the main weapon was the dependency created by the debt, which translated into pressure on the Greek authorities to implement austerity measures

---

Kouvélakis, *La Grèce, Syriẓa et l'Europe néolibérale. Entretiens avec Alexis Cukier*, Paris: La Dispute, 2015.

2   See Chapter 2 above. Cf. also Céline Barbier, 'Ordolibéralisme et économie sociale de marché: la voie allemande de l'Europe?', European Social Observatory, urlz.fr/37ZI.

completely incompatible with the commitments made by Syriza.

The 'sovereign debt' crisis in Europe has demonstrated the political efficacy of such dependency. Obviously, debt is an economic means of extracting and transferring wealth to lenders and, in the event of a risk of default, imposing the solutions most advantageous to them. But it is much more than that. It is a formidable means of *government*. We know that EU policy is largely guided by Germany and France – the countries whose banks were most exposed to Greek debt because they lent recklessly to households, businesses and the state in order to finance their own exports.[3] German and French enterprises were deluged with Greek government orders for technological goods and top-of-the-range military equipment. Gaël Giraud has pointed out the terms of the equation: the volume of loans to Greece by foreign banks quadrupled between 2000 and 2007. He also highlights the use of these sums: 'Greece, that European superpower, was one of the five largest arms importers in Europe between 2005 and 2009. The purchase of fighter aircraft alone (including twenty-five Mirage 2000s from France) represents 38 per cent of its total imports.'[4] To this old source of Greek debt we must add the massive, ongoing flight of Greek capital to German and Swiss banks, whose

---

3   Readers are referred to the report of the committee for the truth about Greek government debt coordinated by Éric Toussaint: CADTM, *La vérité sur la dette grecque. Rapport de la commission pour la vérité sur la dette publique grecque*, Paris: Les Liens qui libèrent, 2015. For a summary of the report, see urlz.fr/37ZN.

4   Gaël Giraud, *L'Illusion financière*, Paris: Éditions de l'Atelier, 2014, p. 38.

volume exceeds the current total debt. Finally, much of the debt is attributable to two series of causes that are invariably concealed: the drain operated by creditors in the form of high interest rates, and fiscal measures greatly advantageous to Greek oligarchs, which reduced tax receipts from 2000.[5]

How, then, can a veil be drawn over the inter-oligarchic system of interests which generated the initial monstrous debt, other than by creating the impression that the situation is attributable exclusively to the incompetence of irresponsible peoples who need to be disciplined and punished? The pressure put on the countries of Southern Europe and Ireland (the famous 'PIIGS') takes on a moral cast. The rulers of the creditor countries explain to public opinion that everyone is duty-bound to pay their debts.[6] This moral crusade is based on a historical falsification of reality. It aims to make people forget the origin of the 'sovereign' debt – an effect of the asymmetrical relations between 'core countries' and 'peripheral countries',[7] and the fruit of a European monetary policy highly advantageous to high incomes and large fortunes, but also, more directly, the result of the financial crisis.[8] The truth is that the 'new

5   See Michel Husson, 'Grèce: pourquoi une dette à 100% du PIB avant la crise?', urlz.fr/37ZS.

6   We must not forget that the private credits held by European banks have been transferred to public European institutions, thus de facto making EU taxpayers shoulder responsibility for any partial or total default.

7   Noëlle Burgi, Introduction, *La grande régression. La Grèce et l'avenir de l'Europe*, ed. Noëlle Burgi, Bordeaux: Le Bord de l'eau, 2014.

8   For a historical analysis of the debt, see Benjamin Coriat and Christopher Lantenois, 'L'imbroglio grec. La dette souveraine grecque prise au piège de la zone euro', urlz.fr/37ZV.

European governance' has introduced an unprecedented model of 'sovereignty' under constant surveillance.

A New Conception of 'Sovereignty'

It has rightly been said that the European Union succeeded in breaking Syriza's determination to reject austerity policies and thereby managed to reverse the verdict of universal suffrage, which had expressed a desire to obtain debt relief. The policy was not entirely new, but formed part of a supervisory regime that commenced before January 2015. From the start of the 'euro crisis' in 2010, European oligarchs were open about it: liberal democracy of the classical kind is no longer suited to a world involved in a generalized economic and military war. The events that have unfolded over the last five years in Greece are of the utmost importance for understanding this strategy. Yanis Varoufakis has made the essential points: 'Greece is a battlefield on which a war against European democracy, against French democracy, has been tried and tested ... I am here because our Athens Spring was crushed, like the one in Prague. Not by tanks, obviously, but banks. As Bertolt Brecht said: "Why send assassins when we can employ bailiffs?" Why stage a coup d'état when you can send the president of the Eurogroup to tell the finance minister of a newly elected government, three days after he takes office, that he has a choice between the previous austerity programme which plunged the country into an enormous depression or closure of its national banks?'[9] Such blackmail, in practice excluding any

9   Quoted in Christian Salmon, 'Rencontre avec Yanis Varoufakis: "Il

rupture with the logic of austerity, was employed in the first accord of 20 February between the Eurogroup and Greece.

But the 'war on democracy' is not restricted to Greece. What is happening to Greece encapsulates in particularly brutal fashion the way that neoliberalism is imposing itself in a large number of countries today.[10] As a matter of urgency, liberal democracy, with its regular elections and more or less changeable public opinion, debates and protests, must be curbed, if not hollowed out, in the 'serious' world of the market economy. Jean-Claude Juncker, the then president of the Eurogroup, was the first to admit this in the German magazine *Focus* in July 2011: 'Greece's sovereignty will be enormously restricted' as a result of the 'future wave of privatizations'. And he added: 'It would be unacceptable to insult the Greeks, but we must help them. They have said that they are ready to accept the eurozone's expertise.'[11] In diplomatic terms, this amounted to saying that a member of the EU, and not the least significant of them symbolically, no longer qualified for democracy, but must be placed under supervision by the inter-governmental and international organizations that make up the 'Troika'. Such supervision has loomed over Greek institutions ever since. Its initial major display of power came in December 2011 with the replacement of Prime Minister George

est temps d'ouvrir les boîtes noires"', Mediapart, 30 August 2015. Readers are also referred to the speech made by Varoufakis on 31 August 2015 during the Rose Festival at Frangy-en-Bresse, *Notre printemps d'Athènes*, Paris: Les Liens qui libèrent, 2015.

10   Yanis Varoufakis, *Le Minotaure planétaire. L'ogre américain, la désunion européenne et le chaos mondial*, Paris: Éditions du Cercle, 2014, p. 19.

11   'Pour Juncker, la Grèce devra se résoudre à perdre une grande partie de sa souveraineté', *Le Monde*, 3 July 2011, urlz.fr/3805.

Papandreou by Lucas Papademos, confidant of the banks and markets, and hitherto governor of the Greek Central Bank. Papandreou's fault, committed at the end of October 2011, was to have proposed a referendum on the structural adjustment plan imposed on him by Merkel and Sarkozy. One of the novelties highlighted by the 'Greek crisis' is that there is no longer any need to respect the conventions when it comes to counteracting liberal democracy. Candour is now the rule in European leaders' statements. In an article in which he conveyed his 'vision for Europe', Jean-Claude Trichet, former president of the ECB, declared that in future 'the authorities in the eurozone would play a much more radical and authoritarian [*sic*] role in formulating states' fiscal policies'.[12] In other words, the form of power over the Greek budget inaugurated by the Troika's directorate would be generalized and become a normal principle of government or, at any rate, a 'legal' form of intervention in the event of a country's rulers not being able or willing to respect the constitutional norm of the fiscal 'golden rule'. National institutions and elected representatives would thus no longer have any choice but to approve the decisions taken by the new authorities – the European authorities reserving the right to exercise sovereign power in the event of 'deviations'. Extrapolation? Let us read the rest of Trichet's statement: 'This separates us from the current framework, which leaves all decisions in the hands of the country concerned. On the contrary, in some cases it would be possible and even obligatory [*sic*] for

12   Jean-Claude Trichet, 'Une vision pour l'Europe', *Les Échos*, 28 December 2011.

the European authorities to take decisions directly.' Trichet is not unaware of the gravity of his suggestion and accepts full responsibility for it: 'Implementing this idea also requires adopting a *new concept of sovereignty*, given the complex interdependence between the countries of the eurozone.'[13] When we recall that one of the oldest historical pillars of liberal democracy is the principle of 'no taxation without representation', we can appreciate the historic shift effected by the European oligarchs in public law.

The constitutionalization of competition, balanced budgets and monetary policy in treaties is insufficient. New *methods of government* must also be put in place that will override national political authorities in implementing European decisions. In other words, in the event of a serious crisis, economic 'constitutionalization' must be augmented by *direct government* of a member-state by economic and financial authorities arrogating to themselves the right to change or promulgate that country's laws. While this executive policy obeys no pre-set rule, and while the entities that implement it (the Troika and the Eurogroup) do not possess a clear legal status but are equipped with opaque powers,[14] their mission is patent: saving the system of private and public financial interests and keeping national governments on the path of austerity. We can now better

---

13   This 'new concept' simply reiterates the sovereignty of the guardians of the 'economic constitution' discussed in Chapter 2.

14   This is why Jens Weidmann, president of the Bundesbank, argued for the creation of an independent authority responsible for monitoring budgets and debts: 'Sovereignty, he explains, must no longer allow member-states to evade their fiscal responsibility'. See Weidmann, 'Renforçons la surveillance budgétaire au sein de l'Union européenne', *Le Monde*, 1 October 2015.

appreciate Juncker's comments, cited at the start of Chapter 4, which were made on the morrow of Syriza's victory and occasioned controversy: 'To say everything is going to change because there is a new government in Athens is to take one's desires for reality ... There cannot be a democratic choice against the European treaties.'

Whatever It Takes

There was no concerted plan to destroy the most basic principles of classical democracy. Theorization of the new 'sovereignty' simply caps political supervisory practices which European institutions, the IMF and the governments of various member-states had established without bothering unduly about respect for European law. For the sacrosanct 'respect for the rules' invariably brandished by ordo-liberals is blithely violated when it comes to the means employed. Here *anything* is permitted. The history of the 'Troika' or 'Eurogroup' – institutions without any legal standing[15] and without explicit principles – is evidence enough. Greece has been the principal 'laboratory' of the new, authoritarian method of government through debt.[16] As we have seen, this obviously stems from the size of its debt as a proportion of GDP. But the lesson to be drawn applies to all other

---

15   To Yanis Varoufakis, who expressed his surprise at the lack of any notes and minutes, the chair of the Eurogroup, Jeroen Dijsselbloem, openly replied that the Eurogroup did *not* exist in European law, so that its chair could do as he liked (cf. 'Face à la rédaction de Mediapart', 25 September 2015).

16   On the shock doctrine and Greece as a neoliberal laboratory since 2012, see Stathis Kouvélakis, 'Grèce, destruction programmée d'un pays', interview with Jérôme Vidal, *La Revue des livres*, no. 4, March–April 2012.

countries. It indicates the possibility of taking control of a national economy and society by means of debt and, in concrete terms, through a financial blockade mounted by the creditors whom it is meant to legitimize. The three 'loans for reforms' memoranda that Greece has had to sign since 2010, without being in a position to negotiate them, are the most tangible proof, along with the methods employed by creditors to impose their analyses and decisions as well as to control the country's political institutions: visiting ministries regularly, drafting legislation and decrees, drawing up the list of privatizations, directly controlling the civil servants responsible for government receipts, and so on. The means employed by the creditor institutions were even more violent when they encountered resistance from the Tsipras government as it attempted to negotiate, 'calmly' and 'reasonably', a 'more intelligent' policy facilitating absorption of the effects of austerity and a resumption of investment and growth in Greece. They did not hesitate to initiate financial asphyxiation of the country from the beginning of February, two weeks after Syriza's victory, and then to apply it radically from late June and early July 2015, when the ECB decided not to raise the ceiling on the emergency liquidity available for Greek banks but to strangle the economy. The third memorandum of 13 July 2015, which put a noose around Greece's neck, made it perfectly clear that Parliament was no more than a body for registering the instructions of creditors, to the extent that it forced the government to retroactively cancel laws voted since the February accord. Thus, it was stipulated that 'the government must consult the institutions and agree with them on any legislative plan in the areas concerned, with an appropriate period of notice, before submitting it to public consultation or Parliament'.[17]

If we are to believe Varoufakis's insider testimony, the political issue was in fact much more important than the economic issue, which scarcely interested his interlocutors in the Eurogroup. During one meeting, Wolfgang Schäuble, the German economy minister, allegedly said: 'Elections cannot change anything. If the rules changed every time there's an election, the eurozone couldn't function.' To which Varoufakis replied: 'If it's true that elections can't change anything, we should be honest and say so to our citizens. Perhaps we should amend the European treaties and insert a clause suspending the democratic process in countries obliged to borrow from the Troika. But is Europe okay with that? Did our peoples vote for that?'[18] The question would seem to have gone unanswered. But it was enough for Varoufakis to observe that all the participants in the Eurogroup concurred in their contempt for the universal suffrage of a member-state. As we saw in the previous chapter, this is not new: Europe advances by riding roughshod over the rules of electoral democracy.

A Logic of Political War

What, then, is the implacable logic of the Troika? Financial blackmail certainly ensures a real appropriation of wealth

---

17   Declaration of the eurozone summit, 12 July 2015, in Kouvélakis, *La Grèce, Syriza et l'Europe néoliberale*, appendix 3, pp. 205–6.

18   Salmon, 'Rencontre avec Yanis Varoufakis'.

for creditors, but at the same time causes escalating indebtedness, or a kind of large-scale banking 'pyramid scheme' where new loans essentially serve to meet the repayment deadlines on old ones. The third memorandum of July 2015 caused the debt to climb above 200 per cent of Greek GDP.[19] In this sense, from the standpoint of strictly arithmetical rationality, the austerity imposed on Greece is 'irrational'.

Tsipras's initial error was to believe that there was an 'economically rational' way of resisting European diktat and on this same 'rational' basis to hope for balanced mediation at least, if not succour, from Hollande or Renzi.

In reality, the absolute obligation to repay, however absurd and impossible, conforms to a much deeper, political rationality.[20] The members of the Eurogroup cannot have been unaware of this absurdity, even if they had not shown any interest in the social consequences of the measures imposed on the Greek people by the Troika. They are not so stupid as not to have noticed that the debt burden has risen since 2009 (from 115 per cent of GDP to practically 200 per cent in 2016). Even the IMF, an apologist for austerity, ended up seeing this. It was clearly understood by an advisor to the Greek government who followed the negotiations with the Troika closely: 'We set out for battle thinking we had the same weapons as them. We underestimated their power. It's a power that forms part of a veritable social fabric, the way

---

19   Romaric Godin, 'Grèce: la vraie nature du troisième mémorandum', *La Tribune*, 15 July 2015.

20   See Étienne Balibar, Sandro Mezzadra and Frieder Otto Wolf, 'Le diktat de Bruxelles et le dilemme de Syriza', in *Europe, l'expérience grecque. Le débat stratégique*, eds Alexis Cukier and Pierre Khalfa, Bellecombe-en-Bauges: Éditions du Croquant, 2015, p. 51.

people think. It's based on control and blackmail. We've got very few levers in the face of it. The European edifice is Kafkaesque.'[21] Basically, Syriza's programme, presented in September 2014,[22] which had dared to display independence from the *political line* of the Commission, the ECB and the IMF, was the real target of the blackmail. The Eurogroup could not tolerate the implementation of any of the programme's four pillars – as Greek negotiators learnt to their cost. 'Dealing with the humanitarian crisis, reflating the real economy, restoring jobs and labour law, and a civic overhaul of the state and institutions' – all these points in Syriza's programme betrayed a heresy that had, at any cost, to be eliminated from the European Union before any pernicious ideas about social justice became contagious and spread.

'Debtocracy', or, The Sovereign Power of Creditors

Indebtedness has made it possible, provisionally perhaps, to neutralize all the Greek government's efforts to depart from ordo-liberal orthodoxy. Many historical and ethnological traces of debt as a method of enslavement exist.[23] It has even been a direct cause of slavery in certain times and places. In particular, we are familiar with the significance of the ban introduced by Solon on making people surety for loans. Aristotle tells us that the measure to cancel debts, private and public alike, was called *seisachtheia*, or 'shaking

---

21 Christian Salmon, 'Un insider raconte. Comment l'Europe a étranglé la Grèce', Mediapart, 7 July 2015.

22 Cf. urlz.fr/380n.

23 Alain Testart, *L'esclave, la dette et le pouvoir. Études de sociologie comparative*, Paris: Éditions Errance, 2001.

off the burden', precisely because the burden of debt was shaken off thus.[24] Today, financial debt no longer entails an appropriation of individuals by creditors, but it does result in a rich cultural inheritance being made to function as security, in deductions from the flow of new wealth, and in a loss of collective autonomy.

The current situation must be analysed predominantly in terms of power relations. Private lenders are now the real masters of the game by virtue of their key role in financing states. With the backing of ratings agencies, they have acquired the power to guarantee (or decline to guarantee) the continuity of economic life and hence social existence. They are in a position to speculate via derivative products on the ability to repay debts, causing interest rates to fluctuate in line with 'market opinion' about government policy. The power of the financial oligopoly manifests itself in the capacity to oblige states to transform the private debts accumulated on bank balance sheets – debts that have become toxic as the insolvency of private and public borrowers grows – into government debt guaranteed by taxpayers in the last resort.[25] Similarly, the risks taken by banks are ultimately covered by states which, unilaterally or conjointly, recapitalize private banks out of state budgets.

The power of creditors explains why the 'Keynesian pact' (Krugman) of reflation through public expenditure and capital controls no longer works, and why government ministers take absurd measures that serve only to deepen

24   Aristotle, 'The Constitution of Athens', in *The Politics* and *The Constitution of Athens*, p. 214.
25   See Chapter 1 above.

recession. 'Fear of speculators' is the basic reason for austerity policies. In other words, the sovereignty of creditors, acknowledged in practice, leads to a logical inversion of macroeconomic policies.[26] In Latin America, Asia and Europe, self-induced speculative attacks have done such economic and social damage in recent decades that governments have been led to adopt policies contrary to 'good sense' just to 'restore the confidence' of financial markets – those capricious, sheep-like, perverse entities ever ready to increase the risk premium on loans. This obsession with 'confidence' has (Krugman points out) had the effect of making economic policy 'an exercise in amateur psychology, in which the IMF and the Treasury Department tried to persuade countries to do things they hoped would be perceived by the market as favorable'.[27]

'Restoring market confidence': this is the key to the Washington Consensus and its structural reforms. Such is also the *ne plus ultra* of European policy, which merely 'copies and pastes' IMF recipes from the 1980s and 90s. This elegant phrase is simply a euphemism for states' self-subjugation to the power of finance. Competition between speculative funds and between banks results in uncontrolled risk-taking and behaviour that fuels bubbles, stokes over-indebtedness and, ultimately, creates the domino effects of the financial crisis.[28] Competition between financial centres

---

26 Paul Krugman, *The Return of Depression Economics and the Crisis of 2008*, New York: W. W. Norton & Company, 2009.
27 Ibid., p. 106.
28 Heightened competition between financial actors is a key factor in bankers' 'myopia about disaster'. See Laurence Scialom, *Économie bancaire*, Paris: Éditions La Découverte, 2013, p. 73.

leads them to align themselves with the countries that practice the lightest regulatory touch, in the manner of the City
and, more generally, Anglo-American finance. This suits
the financial actors of other countries fine, because they
derive juicy remuneration from it.[29]

But 'restoration of confidence' is above all an expression
of the relations between a 'debtor state' and the powers that
lend to it under conditions dependent on this famous 'confidence'. Thus, in and through their fiscal policy, neoliberal
states have constructed their own subordination to markets,
which are in a position to dictate the policy they must follow.
Hence the spiral of concessions and presents to the wealthiest classes and companies. Wolfgang Streeck justifiably
compares the way that shareholders are guaranteed control
of the boards of directors of private enterprises, in order to
ensure a favourable distribution of profits, with the way that
banks and hedge funds have taken control of governments
to secure tax benefits and access to public property: 'Much
as an increase in shareholder value requires management to
hold down the workforce or – better still – to lock it into
common efforts to boost the share price, so does the trust
of creditors require that governments persuade or compel
their citizens to moderate their claims on the public purse
in favour of the "financial markets"'.[30] This also confers
considerable power on the public servants who negotiate
the debt in bond markets. The Greek example demonstrates
that the rights of loan capital now prevail *absolutely* over the

---

29   See Jean-Michel Naulot, *Crise financière. Pourquoi les gouvernements ne
font rien*, Paris: Éditions du Seuil, 2013, p. 73.
30   Streeck, *Buying Time*, p. 80.

right of populations to basic guarantees and quality public services. In other words, the debtor state must above all ensure the *welfare of capital* against its population.

Societies Enslaved to Debt

How are deductions from the wealth produced to repay the debt, at least in part, to be ensured? And how is a situation to be created where this draining of wealth from debtor to creditor lasts long enough to avoid unduly heavy losses for lenders in the event of over-indebtedness? With the Greek case, this classical problem has taken an exemplary turn. The objective of the 'loans for reforms' accords was not only to 'suck out' wealth, but also to reorganize society – that is, to impose reforms, especially as regards privatization, wages and the labour market. What is striking about the current domination of finance is the ability acquired by financiers to use blackmail to dictate major economic, social and political changes to the benefit of local oligarchies. Any protocol, pact, contract or memorandum affords an opportunity to attach 'conditionalities' to loans to a government that urgently needs funds, to prevent its economy being strangled and its society descending into chaos. This blackmail is not to be confused with a much subtler mode of governmentality, relying on individual management of human capital.[31] We are dealing with two different ways of 'governing by debt'. In the case at hand, government debt does not introduce a subjective relationship of

---

31   A confusion displayed by Maurizio Lazzarato in *Governing by Debt*, South Pasadena: Semiotext(e), 2015.

accumulation and profit, in the manner of a student loan, as a putative anticipation of the income derived from the 'human capital' built up in studies. Instead, government debt introduces a blackmail relationship of the 'repayment or your life!' variety. It is not so much a biopolitics as a 'necropolitics'.[32] It consists in the fact that the creditor has power of life and death over a banking system, a productive apparatus, a government and, ultimately, a population.

In the end, the *conditionality* of the loan is more important than the *sustainability* of the debt when it makes it possible to impose 'structural reform'.[33] If the Organization for Economic Co-operation and Development (OECD) is to be believed, such reform seeks to remove obstacles to international trade, to attract direct foreign investment and to liberalize financial markets. More broadly, it aims to lower wage costs in production to improve competitiveness, make labour markets flexible, reduce public expenditure and cut pensions − in a word, to 'free up economic supply' from any constraint deemed excessive by employers.[34] Radical transformation of the most indebted countries via their 'subjection to a programme' has become the main objective of the European Commission and the 'apolitical' ECB.

The OECD proposes directions for use of the debt crisis. The text just cited explains very clearly that 'structural reform' encounters social and moral resistance, especially

---

32   See Achille Mbembe, 'Nécropolitique', *Raisons politiques*, no. 21, January 2006.
33   See CADTM, *La vérité sur la dette grecque*, Chapter 5, 'Les condition-nalités, ennemis de la soutenabilité'.
34   OECD, 'Le chemin sinueux de la réforme structurelle', *L'Observateur de l'OCDE*, no. 261, May 2007, urlz.fr/380z.

when it comes to liberalizing labour markets. What the OECD calls the 'political economy of reform' is simply a set of methods for successfully imposing it in the face of 'established interests, the anxieties of workforces, or deep-rooted institutional arrangements that are difficult to alter'. Actors should not shrink from a policy of making things worse to further their ends: 'Major crises are not comfortable for political leaders, but *they can foster change*. Studies by the OECD indicate that an output gap (the difference between actual and potential output) of 4 per cent increases the likelihood of a major structural reform by nearly one-third. It was a crisis, marked by a recession, a descending wages spiral and sizeable deficits, which prompted change in the Netherlands in the 1980s, and in Canada and Finland in the 1990s, when the public finances were in deadlock. Economic gloom also imposed reforms on Japan. The case of Europe is instructive. The countries that have carried out radical and difficult reforms, like Denmark, Ireland, the Netherlands and the UK, *indicate the importance of crises in eliciting support for reforms and advancing them.*'

Thus, in order to impose 'internal devaluation' of incomes, especially civil service pensions and salaries, it is necessary to cleverly exploit debt and currency crises to get the reforms accepted by public opinion as so many measures for the 'common good'. Above all, however, a population must deliberately be put 'under stress', in a situation of acute crisis, so that it ends up accepting, albeit with a heavy heart, the erosion of its political gains and social rights. People have quite rightly denounced the 'illegitimate' character of debt, demonstrated its 'odious' character, and exposed the violations of the most basic human rights entailed in its repayment.[35] It is right – and will continue to be right – to show that the consequences of the memoranda of agreement for which the lenders are jointly responsible contravene the European Social Charter. But there is one thing that must be grasped above all else: debt is one of the most effective *weapons of political war*. The OECD puts it bluntly: 'Economics rarely decides the outcome of the battle of reforms: it is politics that holds the key.'

Truth sometimes emerges from the mouth of the Eurocrats themselves. A few days after Syriza's victory, the chair of the Eurogroup, Jeroen Dijsselbloem, stated: 'Either you sign the memorandum or your economy is going to collapse. How? We are going to crash your banks.'[36] We can see why Varoufakis could claim that there was never any negotiation between Greece and the Eurogroup, only 'match-fixing'.[37] The only possible outcome was an act of surrender. In the Greek case, this took a while to materialize, due to Syriza's victory and six months of resistance by the Tsipras government. Such blackmail has virtually become a habit. Cyprus had already paid the price in 2013, as had Ireland in 2010. Trichet even dared to threaten the Irish government with 'exploding a bomb in Dublin' should the government not repay all its creditors.[38] Tsipras

---

35   See *La vérité sur la dette grecque*, p. 115ff.

36   Salmon, 'Un insider raconte'.

37   'Yanis Varoufakis: pour une nouvelle dissidence européenne (2)', interview with Christian Salmon, Mediapart, 22 September 2015, and 'Rencontre avec Yanis Varoufakis'.

38   Romaric Godin, 'La BCE a-t-elle menacé l'Irlande d'une "bombe" en 2011?', *La Tribune*, 11 September 2015.

assumed the role of leader of a small member-state anxious to obtain a goodwill gesture from 'friends' with whom he had cultivated 'relations of trust'. This was to misread the political determination of Syriza's enemies, who asked the ECB to cut liquidity to Greek banks, thus prompting their bankruptcy and economic collapse. Unless Syriza had repudiated the second memorandum after the victory of January 2015, rather than continuing to meet the deadlines for repayment of an unsustainable debt, exhausting available resources, the room for manoeuvre was non-existent.

In the absence of a clean break, the Greek government was on the back foot until the surprise announcement of a referendum at the beginning of July, which offered the glimpse of a change in the balance of forces. With the benefit of hindsight, it seems to have been a fool's game.[39] The lesson of Greece is that *no real change of direction can come from within the European institutional mechanism*, because of the blackmail used against those who resist the dominant line. The threat of 'Grexit' brandished by Wolfgang Schäuble on 11 July, with the support of an ECB encouraging a run on the banks, was merely the latest bluff to force the Greek Left back into line. With this increasingly explicit and aggressive blackmail, Europe's leaders achieved their ends: eliminating the Greek anomaly by converting the wolf into a lamb. The point was to make an example, to demonstrate the price of disobedience to other countries that might be tempted to escape the austerity trap – Portugal or Spain, for example.

---

39 On this point, see the convincing demonstration by Alexis Cukier, 'Après la défaite de Syriza', in *Europe, l'expérience grecque*.

But we must not isolate the 'Greek crisis' from the 'European crisis' or the 'global crisis'. They are aspects of a generalized war to change the world in accordance with the norms of capitalist rationality. The policy of the major Bretton Woods institutions and the US government has constantly been orientated to negating democracy, supporting dictatorships and despotic regimes, and participating in coups d'état in Latin America.[40] With the Washington Consensus, implemented since the 1990s, the objective remains the same, but the methods have changed somewhat. Pressure has become indirect, utilizing the debt weapon. Why establish a military dictatorship if the same outcome can be obtained via markets? Submission to power is replaced by 'compliance with agreements', on pain of economic and financial strangulation. Neoliberalism continues to be imposed on societies, which it transforms using economic blackmail. The ongoing war waged by creditors is conducted by all available means: blackmail over jobs, financial strangulation, and fear of privatization. The term given it acts as a mask: 'the crisis'.

We must draw some political conclusions from Syriza's defeat. Its leadership did not have an adequate appreciation of the character of the situation, the strength of the opponent, or the objectives and tactics needed to fight him. It remained profoundly *conciliatory*. It believed it could pull through by adjusting, inflecting and re-orientating public policy; it still does. It does not grasp the underlying logic of the European Union and does not appreciate the

---

40   See Éric Toussaint, *Banque mondiale, le Coup d'État permanent. L'agenda caché du Consensus de Washington*, Paris: Syllepse, 2006.

resolve of its adversary. The major strategic error committed by Tsipras and the majority leadership of Syriza was to believe they could persuade an interlocutor in good faith, with rational arguments, to avoid an open crisis with the European Union. But persuading the Eurogroup of the terrible consequences of prolonging austerity assumed that Europe was a 'Habersmasian' universe where the ethical rule of rational public discussion prevailed. This is also the error of Stiglitz, Krugman or Piketty, who stride onto the historical stage armed with the majestic scientific truth which they believe invincible. Faced with the *iron system* of oligarchic interests, neither good faith nor the power of rational argument carries much weight. The war waged on Syriza by the European Union has demonstrated that no 'social' adjustment of austerity can be envisaged in the current framework of the eurozone and the treaties. But it has also exposed the inanity of political conduct that consists in pledging adherence to that framework while wishing to avoid suffering its consequences. The indispensable confrontation with the ordo-liberal European Union obviously calls for tactical and technical measures to avoid a social disaster on the scale of an isolated country. And this confrontation is at the heart of any alternative strategy.

6

The Neoliberal Oligarchic Bloc

The current reinforcement of neoliberalism is not the result of some theoretical error or the propagation of 'false ideas'. No intellectual magisterium will ever be enough to put the world to rights. Keynes was wrong to claim one-sidedly that 'soon or late, it is ideas, not vested interests, that are dangerous for good or evil.'[1] To understand *neoliberalism in action*, we must examine the collective forces and particular oligarchies pursuing it. The question is how a sufficiently powerful coalition crystallized to impose this logic as the sole acceptable 'reality'. There can be no reinforcement of neoliberalism without a coalition of different groups, and no coalition without passionate motivation and a mobilizing project. It goes without saying that the formation and

---

1   John Maynard Keyes, *The General Theory of Employment, Interest and Money* (1936), London and Basingstoke: Royal Economic Society/Macmillan Press, 1977, Chapter 24 ('Concluding Notes on the Social Philosophy to which the General Theory Might Lead'), p. 384.

activity of this coalition differ from country to country, depending on the history of national institutions. Here we shall mainly be dealing with the French case.

Agents of Radicalization

We must first rid ourselves of the neoliberal imaginary, which dissolves power into communication networks and institutions into the smooth, flat world of generalized commerce (the overly famous 'global village'). Neoliberalism does not boil down to globalized commodification and anonymous financialization. As a project and system, it has faces and names. It is implemented and legitimized by political groups, social forces, economic powers and media circles, forming a 'new aristocracy', which has already radically subverted democratic principles.[2] Financial capitalism does not only consist of magma flows handled by interconnected computers. It has its institutions, its rules and even its territories. For if the normative logic that has become established on a world scale is embodied by powers with global reach (multinationals, financial actors, international organizations, European Union, etc.), the national powers which implement its norms are as much co-producers as importers.

Let us use the term *neoliberal oligarchic bloc*[3] to designate

---

2   Lionel Jospin adopted the term 'new aristocracy' from Tocqueville to refer to the implicit alliance formed during the 1980s 'between business leaders, financiers, senior managers in industry and services, senior civil servants, and media VIPs': Jospin, *Le monde comme je le vois*, Paris: Gallimard, 2005, p. 163.

3   The term is used to refer to the power structure in Spain in the

this coalition of elite groups, which have specific interests in the various institutions and social sectors where they are dominant, and common interests inasmuch as they can only dominate through the organic solidarity that unites them. This composite power, at once national and international, is jointly ensured by parties, businesses and public institutions. It is embodied and soldered by individuals who circulate from one end of the social sphere to the other, and who seem to be characterized by a social and geographical ubiquity that enables them to mobilize the most varied resources in power relations.[4]

In political philosophy, 'oligarchy' in the singular refers to the class of the wealthy gripped by the demon of limitlessness.[5] When analysing the concrete forms of neoliberal oligarchic power today, it must be used in the plural. Oligarchies are the various powers caught up in the subjective vertigo of accumulation and they are mutually supportive. They legitimize themselves by believing that extreme concentration of wealth and political power in the hands of a small number is the sole guarantee of relative preservation of the welfare of the great majority of the population.

We can distinguish four main components in such power: the government oligarchy and senior bureaucratic caste at

---

late nineteenth century, following the classical analyses by Joaquín Costa (*Oligarquía y caciquismo como la forma actual de gobierno en España. Memoria y resumen de la información*). We are using it in a quite different sense.

4   See Luc Boltanski, 'L'espace positionnel. Multiplicité des positions institutionnelles et habitus de classe', *Revue française de sociologie*, vol. 14, 1973; Anne-Catherine Wagner, *Les classes sociales dans la mondialisation*, Paris: Éditions La Découverte, 2007.

5   See Chapters 1 and 3 above.

the head of states and international organizations; financial actors and the top management of major enterprises wielding increasing corporate power, especially in the financial sphere; the leading opinion and entertainment media, to which we should add counselling and communications professionals; and academic and publishing institutions, as producers and diffusers of the discursive 'cement' of oligarchic power. These components are not all political in the strict sense, but they all play a *political role* without which we cannot explain the current neoliberal radicalization.

The bloc's power stems from its diversity and its dual character, national and international. In it, naturally, we find the principal beneficiaries of the economic system, possessors of considerable private wealth or the most senior private sector executives, who are the other major beneficiaries of shareholder capitalism. But we also find the most senior national and international civil servants, quick to head for the most lucrative posts in financial capitalism, who have a close relationship with professional politicians enjoying the satisfactions of power and sometimes, too, the charms of personal enrichment. Mention must also be made of the political and economic system's media spokespersons – conformist economists and editorialists – mixed with showbiz and sporting idols, who together feed the hypnotic spectacle of a manufactured 'reality'. Not to forget the 'shadowy actors' who manufacture economic models and legal tools facilitating the globalization of markets and the transformation of states into 'agencies' at the service of business. These closely connected hubs, where we often find the same names, the same networks and the same dynasties, possess economic, political, intellectual and media resources enabling them to accumulate wealth and power at the same time.

The dominant oligarchic system has three main features: entrenched self-reproduction of political and economic elites; systemic corruption rooted in 'return favours' and the exchange of 'mutual services'; and dual inscription, national and international, of its power apparatuses. Three factors in the oligarchy's operation work to consolidate this bloc: the neoliberal coherence of government policy, whether right- or left-wing; the professionalization of politics, monopolized by a small oligarchy of unshiftable 'barons' and moonlighters; and the fashioning of 'reality' by the dominant economists and media. The bloc's fragility is the flip side of its strength: the autonomy detaching it from the rest of society. Its confinement within the circular operation of its interests, its economic and cultural internationalization, its profound ignorance of what goes on 'below', and contempt indeed for anyone outside the oligarchic sphere – these strip the 'elites' of all legitimacy in their claim to lead society, and prompt their massive rejection in angry gestures that take unpredictable forms.

Professional Politics and Neoliberal Domination

Professional politics, which dates back to the very beginnings of representative democracy, is a highly effective vector for imposing neoliberalism. Today it is the target of new forces, such as Podemos attacking the 'caste' in power in Spain, and old forces, like the National Front belabouring the 'UMPS'.[6] The very grave crisis afflicting 'representative democracy' today stems from the conjunction of a structural vice – the professionalization of politics or *caciquismo* – and the effects of neoliberal rationality's assault on the great mass of the population. Since the 1980s, the main parties 'of government', whether right-wing or left-wing, have implemented a programme to liberalize financial markets, international trade and the labour market in a constant ratchet. They have done so by exploiting the particular advantages of professional politics, which shield them from the consequences of their own measures and laws. In the face of repeated scandals about tax fraud by elected representatives or government members, the illegal financing of parties, the misuse of company assets, the fixing of public works contracts and the hidden commissions that go with it, the 'nation's representatives' have been forced to introduce certain rules of transparency and caps to elective mandates. But there is still a long way to go.[7] For the most part, the professionalization of politics remains unaffected: the appropriation of power by eternal feudal lords is flourishing, as is the political corruption which forms its inseparable

6   UMPS: a neologism mocking the interchangeability of the main two parties in France: the Union pour un mouvement populaire and the Parti Socialiste (translator's note).

Not only does the National Front not challenge the benefits attaching to representatives' professional duties, it tends to abuse the prerogatives of elected representatives by shielding itself from the most basic obligations of transparency.

7   Michel Pinçon and Monique Pinçon-Charlot have calculated that, out of 297 Socialist deputies, 207 held more than one elected office. On the right the position is worse. Cf. *La violence des riches. Chronique d'une immense casse sociale*, Paris: Éditions La Découverte/Zones, 2013, p. 95.

shadow.[8] Some of those found guilty of fraud and abuses of all kinds calmly continue their political career as if nothing had happened.[9] This is because professional politics is based on a 'hidden electoral property qualification', which affords it comparative shelter from popular protest and which, whatever happens, ensures the political controls remain in the hands of the oligarchic bloc. However, it breeds massive resentment.[10]

The main parties' oligarchies import the imperatives of the new global capitalism into the political arena. The 'national' or 'republican' rhetoric used and abused by French political leaders does little to conceal the transfer of norm creation to *unelected*, inter-governmental or international bodies, operating independently of any control by citizens. The traditional adversarial game between Left and Right has given way to a game of alternation between two fractions of one and the same political and economic oligarchy, unified by the entrepreneurial transformation of the state. Of course, the two fractions of the political oligarchy are not quite identical, for electoral competition presupposes a minimal differentiation of the platforms 'on

8   See Pierre Lascoumes and Carla Nagels, *Sociologie des élites délinquantes. De la criminalité en col blanc à la corruption politique*, Paris: Armand Colin, 2014.

9   See Graziella Riou Harchaoui and Philippe Pascot, *Délits d'élus. Quatre cents politiques aux prises avec la justice*, Paris: Max Milo, 2014; Noël Pons, *La corruption des élites. Expertise, lobbying, conflits d'intérêts*, Paris: Odile Jacob, 2012; Antoine Peillon, *Corruption*, Paris: Éditions du Seuil, 2014; and numerous investigations by Mediapart.

10   See Daniel Gaxie, *Le cens caché. Inégalités culturelles et ségrégation politique*, Paris: Éditions du Seuil, 1978. According to an investigation by Ipsos in 2014, '65 per cent of French people regard most politicians as corrupt. 84 per cent think they mainly act in their own interests.'

offer'. But the distinction is wearing dangerously thin for these parties, and they are losing credibility. The left fraction of the oligarchy is traditionally more liberal in the area of 'values', morals and individual liberties, whereas the right fraction flaunts its conservatism in these domains. But they have long since coincided in their adherence to the same economic *doxa*, as well as more recently agreeing on the pre-eminence of the executive and approving the strengthening of the police's administrative powers at the expense of judicial oversight. Electoral democracy is thereby completely deactivated, reduced to an illusion in a shadow play.

Systemic Corruption

The spectacle of former political leaders like Aznar, Blair, Schröder, Sarkozy, Clinton or Strauss-Kahn using their fame and address book to make a fortune out of lectures and advice to investment funds, banks and large firms, reinforces the rejection of a corrupt caste. Over and above these lucrative conversions, the accumulation of wealth is a powerful oligarchic glue. It is the objective that welds them, the principle that in practice destroys the legal frameworks and regulations which the oligarchs are supposed not only to uphold, but to enforce. To explain the advent of neoliberalism, it is not enough to emulate orthodox Marxists and blame the dominant class's resolve to restore profit margins. In reality, the pursuit of wealth tends to become 'the Law and the prophets', as Marx put it, not only for capitalists, but for all elite groups in their respective fields – politics, art, sport, media, and even areas utterly alien to economic logic, such as higher education. Today, all oligarchies tend to identify with the figures of the 'manager', the entrepreneur, even (in the case of the most uninhibited) the 'billionaire'.[11] The logic of accumulation is even taking root in the state bureaucracy, so obvious has it become that increased 'corporate margins' must govern public policy across the board. Private-sector principles are imposed with the introduction of New Public Management, the development of public–private partnerships, opaque bonus systems, and the outsourcing of expertise and auditing to private companies.

While the interpenetration of the corporate world, the state bureaucracy and professional politics is not a new phenomenon, it has assumed an unprecedented structural character today.[12] The situation may be characterized as *systemic corruption* at every level, from local bodies to the apex of the state. Where once it could be said that in 'the modern age', on account of 'rapid and constant economic growth', 'the dangers of corruption and perversion were much more likely to arise from private interests than from public power',[13] we have to recognize that those days are well and truly over. Corruption now emanates as much from the public sphere as from private interests.[14] The scandals

11   Thus, Emmanuel Macron declared that 'we need young French people who desire to become billionaires': *Les Échos*, 6 January 2015, urlz. fr/380S.

12   See Geoffrey Geuens, *La finance imaginaire. Anatomie du capitalisme des 'marchés financiers' à l'oligarchie*, Brussels: Éditions Aden, 2011.

13   Hannah Arendt, *On Revolution*, New York: Penguin, 2006, p. 244.

14   See Pierre Lascoumes, *La démocratie corruptible. Arrangements, favoritisme et conflits d'intérêts*, Paris: Éditions du Seuil, 2011.

that regularly erupt in 'democratic' countries, involving political figures, banks, pharmaceutical industries, utilities and construction multinationals, not to mention organized crime,[15] are merely its most blatant aspects. The systemic dimension of corruption, based on generalized collusion between oligarchies, translates into a confusion of roles and interests, into the protection enjoyed by big bosses and bankers regardless of what they do, into financial support for politicians from large enterprises and the media, into group properties in construction, banking or armaments. The bulk of this systemic corruption is covered by state protection that survives alternation in office and by a highly effective *omertà*. Only a few very courageous investigators and whistleblowers break this silence, without always unveiling its systemic character, precisely because they treat misdeeds as 'affairs' or 'scandals'.[16] The new 'welfare state' now looks primarily to the welfare of 'investors', in the official terminology for the wealthy. And when, despite all the protection they enjoy, major banks like HSBC, UBS or Crédit Mutuel are belatedly accused of tax evasion costing the state billions, they get off with fines that are far from equivalent to the loss.

States have fostered globalization without social or environmental norms and, in so doing, allowed a shadow economy to develop composed of shell companies, hedge funds, offshore accounts, and sophisticated judicial-engineering constructs

---

15　See Jean-François Gayraud, *Le nouveau capitalisme criminel*, Paris: Odile Jacob, 2014.

16　See Sophie Coignard and Alexandre Wickham, *L'omertà française*, Paris: Albin Michel, 1999.

that render financial flows utterly opaque. Corruption has become coextensive with the existence of states.[17] The latter have helped the dominant classes to 'neuter taxes' with the aid of tax law professionals, experts in 'niches', and to protect fraudsters by leaving access to tax havens open.[18] The first major cause that began sealing the oligarchic bloc, by knitting together the interests of privileged milieus and professional politics, was the dismantlement of progressive taxation. This facilitated rapid growth in the income of business leaders and shareholders, and the amassing of fortunes by the tiny minority of the ultra-wealthy, initially in the USA and UK from the 1980s onwards. This deliberate policy contributed significantly to state debt, with governments borrowing on the financial markets the sums they stopped raising in taxes. This was a doubly profitable stroke for owners of finance capital: the sums they were no longer paying in taxes yielded them interest payments.

The iron system of neoliberalism thus resulted in a series of political decisions by 'lead' governments. All the rest followed, arguing that it would be suicidal for growth and employment not to conform to these aggressive practices, the only ones that can attract capital and firms, depriving other countries of tax revenue and lowering social standards and wages. The Europe of competition has been a chosen land for this kind of collectively self-destructive practice, as

---

17 See Antoine Garapon, 'La peur de l'impuissance démocratique', *Esprit*, no. 402, February 2014.

18 See Alexis Spire, 'La domestication de l'impôt par les classes dominantes', *Actes de la recherche en sciences sociales*, no. 190, December 2011, pp. 58–71, and Alexis Spire and Katia Weidenfeld, *L'impunité fiscale. Quand l'État brade sa souveraineté*, Paris: Éditions La Découverte, 2014.

indicated by the fiscal pillage practiced by Luxemburg and Ireland. More generally, inter-governmental and international organizations (IMF, WTO or OECD) elevated the 'right to dumping' – social, fiscal and environmental – to the status of a norm, before belatedly trying to limit its most destabilizing effects on the global economy.[19]

The Age of Corporate Power

Giant conglomerates, significantly strengthened since the 1980s by privatization and the 'opening up of markets', dominate national markets and, through the number of their subsidiaries and the volume of their trade, the world economy. They have a political power that stems from their financial might, their sometimes exponential growth (Google, Amazon, Facebook, Apple, etc.), their influence on employment and growth, their collection of data about consumers, their ability to incite competition between social and fiscal legislative regimes to evade taxes, and their corrupting influence on political leaders through forceful lobbying.[20] In this sense, large companies are *full-fledged political actors* that have developed specific strategies for influence, nationally and globally. This entrepreneurial power, known as corporate power in the Anglophone world, commands a comprehensive discourse and a battery

---

19   See Anne Michel, 'Soixante-deux pays s'accordent pour lutter contre l'évasion fiscale des multinationales', *Le Monde*, 5 October 2015.

20   On lobbying in the US, see Robert Reich, *Supercapitalism: The Battle for Democracy in an Age of Big Business*, London: Icon, 2007. For the variety practiced in the EU, cf. Sylvain Laurens, *Les courtiers du capitalisme. Milieux d'affaires et bureaucrates à Bruxelles*, Marseille: Agone, 2015.

of arguments attuned to the 'game' imposed by globalization on its major economic protagonists.

The *globalization game* lends weight to the new international norms of 'governance' that dictate the content of the 'structural reforms' to be implemented. In this respect, neoliberalism is not the political economy of pure, perfect markets associated with neo-classical economists. It is international politics in the service of the large enterprises dominating economies and societies.[21] Financial deregulation, the flexibilization of jobs markets, the lowering of corporation tax and taxes on the highest incomes, the obstacles erected to health reform in the US or the introduction of the Tobin tax in Europe, all the curbs placed on the ecological transition by supporters of 'green capitalism' – these are so many results of the collective action of big businesses capable of acting politically to great effect. They lobby elected representatives and administrators, promise positions and orders, blackmail the authorities over investment and relocation, and finance electoral campaigns and parties.

Corporate political power extends and enhances capital's social power over the organization of work, consumption and lifestyles.[22] The quasi-constitutional principle of 'business competitiveness' now underpins all economic, social, educational and even cultural policy. The symbolic

21   Cf. Stéphane Haber, 'Marx, Foucault et la grande entreprise comme institution centrale du capitalisme', in *Marx & Foucault. Lectures, usages, confrontations*, eds Christian Laval, Luca Paltrinieri and Ferhat Taylan, Paris: Éditions La Découverte, 2015, and Stephen Wilks, *The Political Power of the Business Corporation*, Cheltenham: Edward Elgar, 2013.

22   Mark Hunyadi, *La tyrannie des modes de vie. Sur le paradoxe moral de notre temps*, Bordeaux: Le Bord de l'eau, 2014.

submission of French political leaders declaring their 'love of enterprise',[23] or (when crossing the Channel) their 'love of business', is of the utmost significance. 'I love enterprise': the phrase used by a French prime minister during an employers' meeting should be taken seriously. It attests to the new hierarchical relations between the legitimate sources of power. The shift from love of God and King (His temporal representative) to love of country or nation marked a transition between two political eras. The shift from love of country to love of enterprise, including 'France plc', marks another. As representatives of a supreme authority, the purveyor of 'wealth', 'employment' and 'happiness', business leaders and (via their mediation) shareholders participate directly in determining national policy at the highest level, and inflect international trade rules and national laws in line with their own interests.[24]

Large enterprises have been awarded public service contracts in numerous areas (telecommunications, computing, Internet, research, motorways, health, etc.) and thus exercise a pervasive influence on public action and society. Corporate power comes in two phases. Large businesses are governing institutions in that they possess the ability to inflect government policy. But these governing institutions are themselves governed by shareholders, who are narrowly focused on maximizing share prices and dividends.[25] It is through them that the mimetic, irrational, short-termist

---

23   Manuel Valls, 27 August 2014, at MEDEF's summer university.
24   Cf. Susan George, *Shadow Sovereigns: How Global Corporations Are Seizing Power*, Cambridge: Polity Press, 2015.
25   See Crouch, *Strange Non-Death of Neoliberalism*.

behaviour of financial markets is transmitted throughout the economy, state and society. Far from ushering in a democratic capitalism, pension funds and other savings collectors play a decisive role in centralizing capital. This gives them greater power over corporate boards on account of the cross-ownership and volatility of their shares in large enterprises.[26] The managers of large enterprises have seen their own interests aligned with those of property-owners, especially fund managers, via stock options and other benefits (bonuses, pension pots, etc.), whose value depends on share prices. They have become autonomous to the point where they form a separate caste, ruled by a 'global market of executives' whose pay has nothing to do with that of the wage-earners at the summit of the firms' internal hierarchy.[27] In this narrow but powerful circle, transnational norms are established for salaries and benefits that make these managers bearers of the 'new values' of neoliberal capitalism.

One aspect of corporate power is the aid from which the banking oligopoly has benefited for its development. Liberalization of the financial sector from the 1980s onwards resulted in a hyper-concentration that procures super-profits and encourages dishonest practices by a banking cartel which reckoned itself untouchable. François Morin

26   Cf. Frédéric Lordon, *Fonds de pension, piège à cons? Mirage de la démocratie actionnariale*, Paris: Raisons d'agir, 2000. Recent work on the 43,000 largest firms shows that they are 40 per cent owned by a 'core' of 147 firms with a majority financial stake. See 'Un nœud de 147 sociétés au cœur de l'économie mondiale', *Le Monde*, 28 November 2011.

27   Olivier Weinstein, *Pouvoir, finance et connaissance. Les transformations de l'entreprise capitaliste entre XXe et XXIe siècle*, Paris: Éditions La Découverte, 2010, p. 127.

has exposed the oligopolistic structure of banking globally.[28] A highly concentrated sector in terms of balance-sheet sizes, and closely interconnected, it is especially potent within the system of corporate power. Mega-banks have knitted a web of interests of such density between states, territorial collectivities and multinationals that it has become very difficult to contain the financial control they exercise over the political field. Fraudulent trafficking of the Libor or Euribor interbank rate,[29] organized tax evasion, risk-taking in speculative markets, deliberate lies about the quality of securities sold, and manipulation of derivatives markets – these attest to a sense of total impunity consequent upon the power acquired by the global banking oligopoly in the 2000s.

The seizure of control of political decision-making bodies by groups and individuals closely connected with economic and financial lobbies is one of the most striking aspects of the neoliberal oligarchic system. The abrupt replacement of rulers in Italy or Greece by 'technocrats', who are themselves often former bankers, is indicative of the increasingly direct ascendancy of financial actors over the world of politics. That Mario Draghi, appointed head of the ECB, was a former 'partner' in Goldman Sachs, responsible for sovereign debt at a time when this investment bank was advising the Greek government on how to doctor its accounts, tells us much about European political leaders' complete lack of moral scruples.

---

28   François Morin, *L'Hydre mondiale. L'oligopole bancaire*, Montreal: Lux, 2015.

29   These are the reference rates at which banks lend or exchange currencies and which therefore serve as indices for the totality of credit activities.

The Osmosis of Banks and Senior Civil Servants

It is sometimes thought that the admirable French Republic is immune from the universal ascendancy of finance. This is mistaken: the hard core of the oligarchic bloc is formed by the increasingly close imbrication of the senior civil service and the world of finance, nationally and internationally. Capitalist rationality has taken root at the heart of the state in the name of 'globalization', which has become a kind of self-sufficient abstract reason for legitimation purposes.[30] The ultra-rapid conversion of the senior state bureaucracy to economic and financial globalization attests to the remarkable flexibility of leaders quick to cast aside the idol that previous generations of state administrators affected to worship: public service, the common good, the Republic.

The osmosis between senior civil servants and the economic and financial oligarchy is now such that the latter does not need to intervene directly to advance its point of view. The Court of Auditors, the Budget directorate and, above all, the Treasury shoulder the task of defending economic orthodoxy and corporate interests. The traditional organs of the French state's administrative *dirigisme* have become levers of neoliberal rationality, while also engaging in an ultra-corporatism to preserve their own benefits. Institutions believed to be devoted to public supervision are, in fact, sites of connivance with market finance. This is not a new phenomenon. Yves Mamou demonstrated almost

---

30   Anne-Catherine Wagner, 'Les classes dominantes à l'épreuve de la mondialisation', *Actes de la recherche en sciences sociales*, no. 190, December 2011, p. 8.

thirty years ago that it was not French capitalists who implemented measures to liberalize finance but the Treasury, which was particularly sensitive to competition from other financial centres. The journalist used the formula of 'the Treasury team's state liberalism' to refer to the ideology of this body of civil servants, converted since the start of the 1980s to the new global *doxa*.[31]

This demonstration is more relevant today than ever. 'Bercy' is the name for the inter-state power that has been imposed on all other ministries. It pressured the French government into capitulating to the banking lobby when it came to regulating banking activities, into defending creditors' interests at all costs in the euro crisis, blocking the Tobin tax, and protecting high frequency trading: 'In France, there is no longer an impenetrable barrier between private high finance and public high finance. They are inhabited by the same people, who blithely risk confusing administrative power in the service of the general interest with discretionary power in the service of the banking sector's short-term interests.'[32] One can no longer count the Treasury directors and other personnel, right-wing and left-wing alike, who have moved on to private banks. It is enough to cite the names of Jacques de Larosière, Christian Noyer, Michel Camdessus, Jean-Claude Trichet, Philippe Jaffré and Louis Gallois to register the extent to which their bearers concentrate *both* financial power and political

---

31   Yves Mamou, *Une machine de pouvoir. La Direction du Trésor*, Paris: Éditions La Découverte, 1988.

32   Gaël Giraud, Introduction to Adrien de Tricornot, Mathias Thépot and Franck Dedieu, *Mon amie, c'est la finance! Comment François Hollande a plié devant les banquiers*, Paris: Bayard, 2014, p. 18.

power in their hands.[33] Michel Pébereau, one of the main protagonists in the neoliberal turn of the late 1970s, who subsequently became head of the BNP bank, has been one of the most influential figures in French political economy over the last thirty years – a major promoter of austerity policies and the managerial transformation of the state when head of the Institute of Enterprise, not to mention the influence he enjoyed as head of the governing body of the Institut d'études politiques in Paris (Sciences Po) for a quarter of a century, from 1988–2013.[34]

These senior civil servants have long been closely connected by their membership of ministerial cabinets as well as the boards of large companies, and by their presence within the organizational structures of banks. Their careers, which see them pass from the Treasury to the directorate of large private banks, from the Bank of France to the European Commission, the ECB or the IMF, and vice versa, are enough to show how they form the core of the French, European and, sometimes, global oligarchic system. Thus, Rawi Abdelal has demonstrated the important role of 'French policymakers' in constructing the codes of global finance from the 1980s onwards.[35] The consanguinity of civil service and banks, which is not to be found to the same degree in any other economic sector, helps us understand the internal logic behind the 'single policy' pursued by all governments as regards the concentration of banks or the

---

33 Ibid., p. 140.
34 See Michel Pébereau, *La politique économique de la France*, Paris: Armand Colin, 1986.
35 Abdelal, *Capital Rules*.

remuneration of CEOs. Therewith we can more clearly appreciate what it is, at the heart of the state apparatus, that prevents any serious challenge to the financialization of the economy, painted as an inexorable natural phenomenon. For it is these individuals, wedded to the norms of international finance, who dictate political choices via the oligopoly of private ratings agencies and the IMF. They can assert that what is at stake is the very ability of states to function, with the result that, through their mediation, states incorporate systemic risk by buying private debt securities and making taxpayers accountable for the risks which are actually down to creditors.

Via senior state and banking officials, the imperatives of financial institutions refashion public policy by prioritizing the protection of holders of 'sovereign debt' over any social responsibilities. The banking law of 18 July 2013, designed by Pierre Moscovici and labelled 'for the separation and regulation of banking activities', is typical of the influence of French financial lobbies, which defend the power of large, French-style systemic banks. An alibi law protecting the speculative operations of the four systemic behemoths – BNP, Société Générale, Crédit Agricole, BPCE-Natixis – it deliberately preceded the European process initiated by Michel Barnier to destroy it from within, with German and, naturally, British backing. And when the European Parliament sought to take control of the financial regula-tion dossier, the French government and numerous MEPs, left and right alike, vigorously opposed it.[36] This is because

---

36 See Christian Chavagneux and Thierry Philipponnat, *La Capture*, Paris: Éditions La Découverte, 2014.

it was necessary, in the name of 'economic patriotism', to protect the super-profits of the four French giants – profits only made possible by *public cover* of the risks taken in markets.[37] The lesson of Dexia and the tab of ten billion dollars left for taxpayers to pick up have served no purpose.

Economic Expertise and the Mediatic Shaping of Reality

Kant made it a secret article of his considerations on government: 'The possession of power inevitably corrupts the free judgement of reason.'[38] But the corruption of judgement does not always take the same form. The economic language in which political figures think and express themselves has an insidious corrupting effect, in that it legitimizes purely individual motives for acting, discourages any collective action, and promotes the market as a site of equity and source of prosperity. But what above all characterizes the oligarchic system in this regard is the ban on supposing that a political logic different from neoliberalism could possibly exist. We cannot overlook what the discourse cementing the oligarchic bloc owes to its academic component.[39] Here we need to identify the *political role* of *mainstream* economic expertise when it places itself directly at the disposal of neoliberal governments and uses the media as echo chambers. This public role is denied,

37   Giraud, Introduction to *Mon amie, c'est la finance!*, pp. 10–12.
38   Immanuel Kant, 'Perpetual Peace: A Philosophical Sketch', in *Political Writings*, ed. H. S. Reiss, Cambridge: Cambridge University Press, 1991, p. 115.
39   See Laurent Mauduit, *Les imposteurs de l'économie*, Paris: Pocket, 2013.

and the modelling and mathematizing apparatus of academic economic discourse serves as a convenient cover. However, with their reports, notes and opinions, orthodox economists, empowered by their monopolization of university posts since the 1980s, have established themselves as the main experts in public affairs, be it the environment, teaching, employment, health, the media, or research. The 'scientific authority' they don derives, above all, from the balance of forces in the economic field. Invested thus, they have actively helped determine the intellectual schemas echoed by the media and closed down any real debate on the underlying causes of the 2008 crash, as well as the policies pursued thereafter. Their crude errors before the 2008 crisis have not stopped them – quite the reverse – ruling the roost in the media, universities and among political leaders or bank executives. For several decades, the voice of heterodox, dissident and 'dismayed' economists, however productive, creative and pluralistic, has found it very difficult to make itself heard in scholarly institutions, as well as the media and mainstream politics. The explanation may seem rough and ready, but it corresponds, alas, to the dire reality: mainstream economists, in addition to the academic benefits accruing to them from their conformism, write and say what their sponsors in business circles want to read and hear. In other words, as Paul Krugman has rightly said, it is not merely a matter of scientific error but of 'soft corruption', thanks to which there is a great deal of money to be made.[40] Orthodoxy can pay big dividends.

---

40   Paul Krugman, *New York Times*, 6 December 2010, quoted in Mauduit, *Les imposteurs de l'économie*, p. 13.

The great majority of journalists and editorialists who 'occupy' the broadcasting studios suffer from neoliberal parroting. In this respect, the power of the media, far from exercising some kind of 'counter-power', as a corporate narcissism would have us believe, is an integral part of the oligarchic system. It 'sells' the neoliberal vulgate to public opinion, naturalizes it, and helps radicalize its manifestations by demanding that government 'stay the course' with the 'necessary reform' of society. It is not that the media make it their duty to extol the occupants of official roles, as in an ordinary totalitarian dictatorship or classical authoritarian regime. On the contrary. The 'editocratic' power of the dominant media consists in *bringing government back into line* when it deviates from neoliberal normality, and calling public opinion to order by invoking the 'realism' of 'external constraints' against any hint of dissidence. In this sense, there is indeed a 'manufacturing of consent' to neoliberalism, to adopt a formula from Noam Chomsky.

In Europe, the way the leading media 'covered' the European Constitutional Treaty, austerity policies and, more recently, the euro crisis or the Greek crisis shines a bright light on the integration of the dominant journalistic norm into the system's functioning. The normalizing function of this journalism is not explained solely by criteria of urgency (the news 'scoop') or market compulsions to sensationalism. The ownership structure of the assets of media groups controlled by industrialists or bankers is far more decisive.[41]

---

41 For an illustration of the links between the media industry in the US and the American political world, see Geoffrey Geuens, *Les vieilles élites de la nouvelle économie*, Paris: Presses Universitaires de France, 2011, p. 114ff.

Still, the stranglehold of finance and industry over the media does not explain everything. We must also consider the *structure* of the social and professional relations between politicians, journalists and economists. The same schools, the same ideological reference points, the same company: a whole 'milieu' has formed that supports systemic power and for which the popular classes do not exist – except when they make themselves heard by some improper way of voting, in which case they must be taught a lesson by an appropriate *pedagogy*, so as to come to appreciate the rationality of what causes their suffering.

The journalistic and intellectual oligarchy tolerates a few rare and precious exceptions. Above all, it meets with an internal opposition in media and publishing which plays a valuable role, far beyond that sector alone, in countering the logic of intellectual requisition peculiar to the oligarchic bloc. To castigate neoliberal rationality for its abuses, excesses, conflicts of interest and political lies – manifestations of the systemic corruption of the oligarchies – in the manner of independent, genuinely *critical* journalists, is in this sense to do public health work.

The Oligarchic Bloc and the Right-Wing Left

Once in government, the 'Left' does not even attempt to change things. It follows them, precedes them, or even precipitates them. François Hollande is often criticized for 'betraying' his promises. However, it would not be difficult to show that Hollande and those around him had long since rallied to neoliberalism. Did they not declare as early as 1985 that 'competition is left-wing'?[42] This 'betrayal', which we have seen elsewhere, is in fact simply the clearest demonstration of the political effects of oligarchic domination. It is true that in France the switch in public discourse was abrupt. Scarcely two years after the lyrical flights of Hollande's 2012 Bourget speech, Emmanuel Macron – énarque, inspector of finances, investment banker at Rothschild – became economics minister with the aim of implementing the political line he had helped define at the Élysée, as deputy secretary-general to the president of the Republic.[43] Three years after his victory, more discreetly, Hollande appointed François Villeroy de Galhau – *polytechnicien* and énarque, inspector of finances, and former deputy CEO of BNP Paribas – as governor of the Bank of France. The financial oligopoly had indeed regained its place in the institutions of the Republic – the one it had first acquired under Sarkozy. For, with Hollande, it is this 'new aristocracy' that continues to govern and apply the only policy deemed 'rational' by the senior bureaucratic caste, whatever the human cost. Raymond Barre's competitive supply and strong currency policy remains the *pensée unique* of the whole French oligarchic bloc: its ideological cement. Some journalists and analysts have noted the similarity of this policy orientation to that of the previous presidency.[44]

---

42   Jean-François Trans, *La gauche bouge*, Paris: Jean-Claude Lattès, 1985, Chapter 5.

43   Emmanuel Macron was replaced by Laurence Boone, an economist straight from the Bank of America Merrill Lynch, having learned her trade at Barclays.

44   Samuel Laurent, 'Hollande fait-il de l'économie à la Sarkozy?', *Le Monde*, 15 January 2014. Cf. also Laurent Mauduit's articles on Mediapart.

Once engaged in this infernal ratchet, the neoliberal Left is ineluctably led to call into question everything the historical Left regarded as its achievements. Pensions, the thirty-five-hour week, industrial tribunals, permanent contracts, labour law, public service status – all of it must be refashioned in accordance with the prevailing norm. How to explain this seemingly incomprehensible drift to the many voters who still believe in the Left? In truth, neither individual character, nor good or (invariably) bad faith, count. What matters is the totality of environmental effects, educational matrices and relations of interest that make the oligarchic bloc work. And the 'Left', which must be described as on the Right, is an integral part of it.

Conclusion:
Democracy as Experimenting
with the Commons

It is dark. It may not yet be 'midnight in the century', but
the new century, only just born, has had a very inauspicious
start: intensified nationalism, proudly proclaimed xenophobia, and a bellicose religious fundamentalism whose
most disturbing avatars take the form of a death drive[1] –
phenomena that recall the horrors of the last century in
their most tragic guise. Along the gamut of contemporary
neo-fascism, strange alliances emerge in which the most
unbridled and criminal capitalist instinct mingles with
every kind of identitarian irredentism. Neoliberal globalization, far from giving birth to a world pacified by trade
as the irenic gospel of its preachers would have it, is the
breeding-ground of a sanguinary confrontation between
identities, which reveals religious and market 'fundamen-
talisms' to be complementary versions of postmodern

---

1   In the dual sense of a desire to die and a desire to kill.

reaction.[2] A hankering for origins, a retreat into ethnic community, an absolute submission to transcendence: the *great regression* we are witnessing is pregnant with new disasters. Such is the requisition of thought by the deadliest forms of this regression that we find it extremely difficult to open up to new possibilities, as if we were fascinated by what is worse. However, we have no other choice. For a start, we must lucidly consider the condition to which we have been reduced.

A Historical Crisis of the Left

The so-called governmental Left bears its full share of responsibility for the neoliberal radicalization. Contrary to what it would have us believe, it is not an innocent victim of evil financial markets or some abominable, Anglo-American, ultra-liberal doctrine. Rather than resisting the power of the neoliberal Right, it has scuttled itself, intellectually and politically. When it had a majority in Europe in the late 1990s and early 2000s, some thought that a social and political Europe was finally going to prevail over the 'Europe of the banks'. Alas, the opportunity for a reorientation of European policy was completely squandered by most leaders of 'social democracy'. With Schröder, European solidarity went down the drain and German competitiveness through wage compression and flexibilization of the labour market was the sole priority.[3]

---

2   See Bessis, *La double impasse.*
3   Wanting, like Hollande, to be the French Schröder was the worst form of political apostasy. On this point cf. Guillaume Duval, *Made in Germany. Le*

To understand this alignment, we must go back in time a little. If it has been so easy to impose austerity policies in Europe, the overwhelming culprit is European 'social democracy'. Far from constituting a counterforce, it preferred to ally with the Right. Indeed, it went out of its way to prove even more zealous when it came to transferring the burden of the crisis onto the population by increasing taxes, reducing pensions, freezing civil service wages and attacking labour rights. The governmental Left is thus no longer that force for *social justice* whose objective was civil, political and economic equality and whose motor was class struggle. The Extreme Right needed to do no more than let down its net in abandoned working-class territory to instrumentalize the social anger of a fraction of the popular electorate, directing it against immigrants and a 'system' allegedly stacked in their favour.

The present political rot is a direct result of this reorientation of 'social democracy', but also of the defeats suffered by the social and democratic movement in its opposition to neoliberalism. Coming up against a brick wall, many of its forces have demobilized. Overcome by resentment, part of the left-wing electorate has been captured by an Extreme Right skilfully exploiting an 'anti-system' posture. The operation was considerably facilitated by the Socialist government's explicit rallying to the logic of competitiveness and unbridled securitarianism. Indulging in a toxic one-upmanship out of electoral calculation, a conservative republicanism thus sought to outflank the most hardline Right, and even the Extreme Right, on their right. *Like it*

modèle allemande au-delà des mythes, Paris: Éditions du Seuil, 2013, p. 148ff.

or not, this uninhibited subservience has gradually affected all elements of the Left, so that they appear equally compromised in this turn. It is pointless to comfort ourselves by recalling warnings and criticism from within the Left. What is at stake, to the point where its imminent extinction is no longer unimaginable, is the very existence of the Left – the *whole* Left. Theoretical poverty, intellectual laziness, stereotyped oratory, grandiloquent appeals to rediscover great 'values', and shabby positioning dictated by the electoral timetable are certainly to blame. But more than anything else, the Left is suffering from a *lack of any imaginary*. In this respect, the historical collapse of state communism has made things worse. Yet there is no alternative to neoliberalism except in terms of the imaginary.[4] In the absence of a collective capacity to put political imagination to work, starting with experimentation in the present, the Left has *no* future. The same goes for understanding the nature of the neoliberal imaginary – one of whose most striking forms today is Uberization.

For the remarkable strength of neoliberalism is that it feeds off the reactions it provokes. Why? Because these reactions are precisely no more than *reactions*. Reaction is to be understood here as the opposite of action. It means a response, of a predominantly adaptive kind, to an action. Reaction is not initiative; it draws on what it reacts to. In this sense, it is subordinate to it; and that is why it is passive. The fact that neoliberalism celebrates 'reactivity' is by no means innocent. For neoliberalism, the ability to adapt to a given situation is the cardinal virtue of those exposed to competition, because it makes them internalize competition.

---

4   See Chapter 3 above.

But for those seeking to challenge the system as a whole, such an attitude is intellectually and politically suicidal. The crisis of the Left derives, above all, from its powerlessness to overcome the logic of a purely reactive self-definition. While neoliberalism has been reinforced in and through the crisis, the same cannot apply to those struggling against it. Far from mechanically strengthening them by its profundity, the crisis can only weaken and paralyze them. To create the conditions for a confrontation with this system, the Left must stop being a 'reactive Left'. It must make itself capable of genuine activity. It must retake the initiative. It must directly challenge neoliberalism as a *life form*. It must open up the horizon of a 'good life' without conceding anything to a libertarian pseudo-radicalism that spurns norms and institutions, and with its refusal of any limits on 'desire' consecrates the limitlessness of the market.

But the Left must also stop, once and for all, reducing neoliberalism to 'ultra-liberalism', conceived as a project to undermine states in favour of the market, or even making 'ultra-liberalism' the culmination of neoliberalism left to its own devices. Countering an 'ultra-liberal' project of this variety would involve rehabilitating state power and the prestige of public law. This error is still commonplace. Thus, Alain Supiot refers to an 'ultra-liberal globalization' whose end result would be the 'withering away of the state', therewith amalgamating 'ultra-liberalism' and 'libertarian demands'.[5] This view blinds people to the great phenomenon of recent decades: instead of the withering away of the state,

---

5 Alain Supiot, *La gouvernance par les nombres*, Paris: Fayard, 2015, p. 292.

its profound transformation in the direction not of some straightforward 'restriction of the perimeter of democracy',[6] but of a hollowing out of democracy at the state's instigation.

This is by no means a form of totalitarianism, granted, but it is definitely not the classical *Rechtsstaat* either. And for good reason. The whole register of 'foundations' has switched to competitiveness and security – two principles that are the increasingly open secret of the 'neoliberal constitution'. That is why it is not enough to speak, as did Jacques Rancière some ten years ago, of 'States of oligarchic law'.[7] That they are oligarchic is not in dispute, but whether they are '*Rechtsstaaten*' calls for clarification. According to Rancière, these states are ones where 'the power of the oligarchy is limited by a dual recognition of popular sovereignty and individual liberties'. This definition possibly fits classical liberal democracies, but surely not our neoliberal political systems. In them, 'popular sovereignty' and 'individual liberties' are the constant target of challenges, denunciations and restrictions. It would be more accurate to claim that the oligarchy's power increasingly limits popular sovereignty and individual liberties. Above all, we must not forget that, in the language of the neoliberal oligarchy, the 'rule of law' refers to the *exclusive* superiority of private law and, to go straight to the point, the prevalence of property law.[8] And this is what Rancière identifies when he stresses that 'the social power of wealth no longer tolerates any

---

6   Ibid., p. 263.

7   Jacques Rancière, *Hatred of Democracy*, trans. Steve Corcoran, London and New York: Verso, 2014, p. 73.

8   See Chapter 2 above.

restrictions on its limitless growth, and each day its mechanisms become more closely articulated to those of state action'.[9] In other words, oligarchic states erode the authority of public law to the exclusive advantage of the norms of private law.

The precondition for reconstructing the Left is a correct understanding of the state's active role in the offensive to undo democracy in all its forms, including liberal ones. Mistrust of the state is therefore in order. A basic fiction of *statism*, the 'state as tool' – a lever readily available for public action – serves very conveniently to veil the harsh reality of a state that is no longer a corrector of markets, or even the external guarantor of their operation, so much as a *full-fledged neoliberal actor*. The neoliberal imaginary is not the libertarian utopia. Rather than consign the state to non-existence, it ropes it into the logic of competition – something altogether different. This imaginary will not be thwarted by advocating the 'return' of the State or 'restoration' of the Law. That would simply reinforce its sway. In this sense, the return of nation-state schemas[10] merely betrays the Left's persistent intellectual subordination.

The Experience of the Commons against Expertocracy

How should we set about elaborating an alternative to neoliberalism? A methodological precondition is in order. If the

9   Rancière, *Hatred of Democracy*, p. 95.
10   The recourse to Gramscian categories such as the 'national-popular', developed in a context quite unrelated to the current situation, is one of its most curious aspects.

only genuine challenge to neoliberalism is one that counter-poses new life forms to it, we should look in the first instance to those who are experimenting with such forms. Nothing is to be expected of the parties and apparatuses demanding recognition from the state and anticipating positions and subventions from it. To have any chance of success, the elaboration of an alternative must come from *below* – from citizens themselves. This is not to say that we should simply revive the eighteenth-century phenomenon of '*cahiers de doléances*' (lists of grievances). Far from being reactive, it was actually the latent bearer of an alternative project for reorganizing society. But the grievance was addressed to representatives deemed worthy of being representatives. Our current situation requires us to radically challenge the logic of political representation – first and foremost, in the very way the alternative project is developed. We would lose all credibility if we sought to dissociate the way the alternative is developed from its actual content. If, as we believe, the content must be democracy taken to its logical conclusion, the elaboration of the alternative must *already* consist in experimenting with such democracy – that is, experimenting with a political commons.

Entrusting this task to experts would immediately invalidate any claim to offer a genuine alternative. Worse, it would provide grist to the mill of neoliberalism. As we saw above,[11] neoliberal governance disqualifies electoral democracy in the name of expertise. The experience it calls on is the non-shareable experience of bankers and managers. In

---

11   Chapters 1 and 4.

this sense, neoliberalism involves a *confiscation of common experience by expertise*. Only the experience boasted by experts possesses the value of experience, common experience being dismissed as incompetence. To invoke 'political expertise' against financial–managerial expertise is, whether we like it or not, tantamount to accepting the logic of this confiscation. However, appealing to common experience is insufficient. What matters is not so much rehabilitating common experience as giving full rein to experience *of the* commons – that is, the experience of joint participation in public affairs. At stake is the difference between *what is* common and *the* commons. In this respect, the term 'participatory democracy' is inadequate: *any* democracy is direct participation in public affairs (not merely in the election of representatives). This is precisely the meaning of what we have called the 'principle of the commons'.[12] An experience that is common because it is commonplace is not as such an experience of the commons – far from it. On the other hand, a genuine experience of the commons is amenable to maximum sharing and, in this sense, can become common.

Here we should recall how Athenian democracy guarded against the risk inherent in the political promotion of expertise. Experts had the status of 'public slaves' (*demosioi*), which meant that they were the property of the whole city, not of a private individual.[13] These slaves performed a number of tasks indispensable to the maintenance of civic life: management of the public archives and of the currency,

---

12   See Dardot and Laval, *Commun*.
13   On this point, see Paulin Ismard, *La démocratie contre les experts. Les esclaves publics en Grèce ancienne*, Paris: Éditions du Seuil, 2015.

stocktaking of public property, auditing of acting magistrates, and so on. In a city where the annual replacement of magistrates was practiced, along with the principle of non-iteration for all magistrates selected by lot, these slaves often remained in post for several years, conferring on them a certain power over members of the civic community. By entrusting its administration to experts who took no part in public deliberations and decisions, the city aimed to defend itself against the potential threat to its very existence entailed in a certain expansion of the state. Obviously, such an institution reminds us that in Athens the cost of freedom for some was slavery for others. But it also attests to 'resistance by the community of citizens to the advent of a state conceived as an instance separate from society',[14] or rejection of a political apparatus superimposing itself on the 'originating accord' that founds the community of citizens or *politeia*.[15] If expertise was deliberately excluded from the political field, it was so that the knowledge associated with expertise did not create any entitlement to exercise political power. In this sense, the originality of democracy is that it invalidates Condorcet's jury theorem, according to which the making of a decision is a function 'of the level of expertise of each of the participants in the deliberative process'.[16] The quality of deliberation in an assembly depends not so much on each participant's expertise as on the *pooling of experience* by the mass of non-experts – those who, taken individually, are 'incompetent'.

---

14   Ibid., p. 210.
15   Ibid., p. 213.
16   Ibid., p. 153.

The Strategy of the Democratic Bloc

'How can we win battles if we never fight them on our own ground?' Such is the question posed by Éric Fassin.[17] He goes further: 'It is the ideological collapse of the Left that makes possible the assertiveness of the Right.'[18] What this means is that any alliance with a party whose only social-ist feature is its name has been detrimental to the rest of the Left. It means that the Left's defeats, while invariably the effect of an unequal balance of forces, are also intellec-tual retreats, failures of willpower, conscious submission to the 'reality' manufactured by the oligarchies. The strategic question is two-fold. Firstly, how can disparate forces be unified and concentrated, when the oligarchies are struc-tured by countless ties of sociability and highly potent forms of organization? Secondly, how can struggles on a global scale be coordinated effectively? For, while the oli-garchies have managed to equip themselves with national and international institutions that concentrate their power, in stark contrast to the illusion of an empire with no centre or hierarchy, the forces opposing them find it extremely dif-ficult to conceive and pursue an alternative global policy.

As regards the first part of the question, two grand strategies have been formulated. One – that of Hardt and Negri – consists in banking on the elemental, spontaneous communism of the 'multitude' to constitute it as a politi-cal subject. Its failure, plainly visible today, stems above

---

17   Éric Fassin, *Gauche: l'avenir d'une désillusion*, Paris: Textuel, 2014, p. 36.
18   Ibid., p. 32.

all from its dilution of the dimension of the institution. The latter is arbitrarily reduced to a modality of 'production' – that is, a material process supposed to encompass every dimension of existence in an undifferentiated fashion. Conversely, a second strategy, formulated by Ernesto Laclau,[19] starts out from the fact that the 'people' is not a given but a construction. The point is to determine the character of this construction. For Laclau, in addition to the discursive operation of dividing society into two camps – 'people' and 'power' – 'the symbolic unification of the group around an individuality' is inherent in the formation of a people.[20] More specifically, such symbolic unification is said to derive from individuals identifying with a leader who shares features in common with them, making it possible for him to be both their 'father' and their 'brother'.[21] We might query the possibility of reconciling the condition of such identification with the exigencies of democracy, which involves keeping leaders at a distance by citizens exercising effective control.

Even more important: can the electoral success of Podemos in Spain be interpreted as a confirmation of Laclau's 'populism'? To say the least, there are good reasons for doubting it. With the breakthrough of Ciudadanos, the strategy of 'centrality' (neither Left nor Right), which aimed to divide society into two camps – 'caste' and 'people' – has in fact

---

19   Ernesto Laclau, *On Populist Reason*, London and New York: Verso, 2007.

20   Ibid., p. 100.

21   We are thus dealing with a 'democratic' leader, not a 'narcissistic' leader, approximating to the Gramscian concept of 'hegemony': ibid., pp. 59–60.

failed.[22] The cleavage between 'them' (the caste) and 'us' (the people) has not replaced the division between 'Left' and 'Right'. Podemos has ended up occupying the space of a *left-wing* party capable of harnessing aspirations for radical democracy, and benefiting from the support of forces that articulated them with great consistency (in particular, that of Ada Colau, leader of Barcelona en Comú). In this regard, inscribing social rights in the Constitution, introducing proportionality into electoral law and, above all, establishing a mechanism for recalling heads of government half-way through their mandate – these are so many programmatic demands that have played an important role. In the final analysis, Podemos's political future will depend upon its fidelity to this resolute commitment to democracy. Both the spontaneism of the 'multitude' and the construction of 'populist' reason stumble over the key issue of democracy as an institution run by citizens themselves.

More generally, the question of the *party* as prop for the coalition to be constructed must be posed, without excuses and in the light of past experience. We must put it bluntly: for the imperative of a radical democratic politics, it is the party-form as such that must be openly challenged. Far from being an organizational structure that is neutral in content, this form delineates a specific institution entailing a certain idea of political activity. If we judge it in accordance with the normative conception of the 'general will', there is no doubt that any party is a 'faction', if not 'totalitarian

---

22   In his own way, Pablo Iglesias acknowledges this, in an interview with *New Left Review*, no. 93, May–June 2015, when distancing himself from the schemas of *On Populist Reason*.

in germ and aspiration'.[23] The party emerges as a 'machine for manufacturing collective passion', as the tool for an artificial division of society. But underlying such a critique is a view of the organic unity of society that excludes any pluralism.

We shall arrive at a clearer assessment of this form if we regard it as the form of a *content* constituted in very particular historical conditions. This content is the nation-state as it emerged in the second half of the nineteenth century. Inseparable from that content, parties are devoted to engaging in electoral competition for the exercise of power and have a monopoly on the nomination of candidates for elected posts or government roles. In this sense, they 'cannot be regarded as popular organs, but ... are, on the contrary, the very efficient instruments through which the power of the people is curtailed and controlled' – that is, they are cogs in an 'oligarchic government'.[24] In particular, they are a highly effective instrument for professionalizing politics. It follows that political parties are, by definition, tools for selecting a small number of representatives at the expense of mass citizen participation in public affairs, and hence are *fundamentally oligarchic institutions*. To this congenital vice must be added the effects of neoliberal rationality over several decades. With the extension of neoliberal logic, what Arendt could still deem a 'conspicuous abuse' has become systemic: 'the introduction into politics of Madison Avenue methods, through which the relationship between

---

23   Simone Weil, 'Note sur la suppression générale des partis politiques' (1940), in *Écrits de Londres*, Paris: Gallimard, 1957, p. 126ff.

24   Hannah Arendt, *On Revolution*, New York: Penguin, 2006, p. 261.

representative and elector is transformed into that of seller and buyer'.[25]

That is why it would be utterly ruinous to transform a political movement like Podemos into a centralized war machine sacrificing everything – especially the primacy of the civic 'circles' – to the objective of electoral victory. For this would be to cede in substance to oligarchic logic, imitating the parties that belong to the 'caste' system. On closer inspection, however, it is even more counterproductive to hope for the creation of further Podemoses in Europe by 'exporting' the Spanish 'recipe'.

We must not ignore the special circumstances that made Podemos's breakthrough in the legislative elections possible, and the political victories in Madrid and Barcelona which formed the prelude to it. Everything began with the occupation of the squares in May 2011. Its termination did not betoken the end of the enormous energy accumulated and concentrated in the occupation movement. Quite the reverse, as Amador Fernández-Savater has observed; this energy, 'metamorphosing, spread through the different domains of everyday life':

First, neighbourhood assemblies were created, and then came the surge in defence of public services and public goods. The PAH [Platform for the Victims of Mortgages] developed and multiplied, and thousands of almost invisible initiatives began to proliferate everywhere: co-operatives, urban gardens, time banks, economic community networks, social centres, new bookshops, etc. It can be

25   Ibid., p. 268.

said that the 15M event [15 May is the purported date of the start of the occupation of the squares] covered the whole of society with a kind of 'second skin': an *extremely sensitive surface* in and through which everyone feels what happens to others, strangers, as their own experience ... A space of *high conductivity* where different initiatives proliferate and resonate among themselves without reference to any centralizing instance; a *nameless membrane* where unpredictable, uncontrollable currents of affect and energy circulate, joyfully cutting through established social categories.[26]

To ignore this redeployment of energy from the occupation movement, to sever the birth of Podemos from the 'setting in motion' of society as a whole, would be to miss the crucial point. Thus, any attempt to reproduce the 'Spanish schema' from above is doomed to failure. For what is at stake, beyond the electoral breakthrough of December 2015, is the dangerous pre-eminence of the logic of representation and centralization over the logic of equality in participation, or (in the words once again of Fernández-Savater) the prevalence of the *theatre* over the *skin*. The lesson is clear: in order not to become imprisoned in the theatrical logic of representation, 'we must start again with experimentation at ground level and at the level of ways of life' – that is, it's a matter of 're-opening the skin' by inventing 'new collective practices'.[27]

This is the only way to open new possibilities for governments themselves, loosening the noose in which they

---

26   Amador Fernández-Savater, 'La piel y el teatro. Salir de la política', eldiario.es, 16 October 2015; translated into French by the journal *Ballast* under the title 'Incarner la politique'.

27   Ibid.

all too readily placed their own heads on coming to power, even when motivated by the best of intentions. The case of Greece once again warrants our attention. One of the Syriza government's major weaknesses was that it allowed itself to be imprisoned in the most traditional allocation of roles – precisely the one imposed by the logic of the theatre. The rulers play the role of 'actors' on a stage and solicit the votes of citizens reduced to the equally traditional role of 'spectators' of the political drama. However, thousands of initiatives have sprung from the ruins of the social state, aiming not simply to ensure survival, but to defend ways of life and social existence. Most notably, we find self-managed enterprises, collectives of parents and teachers running crèches, nurseries and neighbourhood schools, the explosion of alternative cultures, health centres combining general practitioners, dentists and psychiatrists, etc. – in short, so many attempts from below to proceed 'without the state, without budgets, without public subsidies and private intermediaries', and deserving encouragement from above.[28] The government would have increased its room for manoeuvre domestically had it relied on such initiatives, and encouraged their coordination and integration into a much broader political project. At stake, over and above the particular Greek situation, is the relationship between government and state. In effect, the neoliberal transformation of the state has now reached the point where a government genuinely concerned with popular sovereignty must dare *to govern against the existing state* and, more precisely, against

---

28   Dimitris Alexakis, 'Grèce: l'invention sous la crise (ressources)', 19 June 2015, Mediapart blog.

everything in the state that pertains to oligarchic domination. But it can only do so if it knows how to appeal to the movements that form, or are liable to form, the 'skin' of society, in order to counter the neoliberal logic of state administration.

As to the second aspect of the strategic question (the coordination of struggles internationally), the answer seems to us to consist in the need to construct an *international democratic bloc*. Not a cartel of parties, like the Left Front in France or Syriza in Greece – forms that have revealed their limits – but a bloc composed of all political forces plus trade-union, community, ecological, scholarly and cultural organizations. These would engage in the anti-oligarchic struggle locally, nationally and internationally on the same platform. The international dimension would not be subsequently added to the national struggle, but would be co-extensive with it. The second lesson to be drawn from Alexis Tsipras's capitulation is precisely that we must beware the illusion that a national electoral victory, even one derived from massive social mobilizations, is enough to change the situation. Once again, the weakness of that government was that it let itself be trapped in a face-off with the Eurocratic oligarchy, without seeking to construct a balance of forces at a continental level.

From this point of view, the call to 'have done with Europe'[29] evinces acute blindness. That it is necessary to make a 'break with the institutional frameworks of actually existing Europe' is something we can readily agree

---

29   Cédric Durand, ed., *En finir avec l'Europe*, Paris: La Fabrique, 2013, p. 149.

with. But should we regard 'the European question [as] secondary'?[30] Is it enough to assert the need to 'start with the essentials in the contemporary crisis', which is purely economic – namely, unemployment, the exhaustion of a mode of development, and the exacerbation of inequalities?[31] In bypassing the political issue of Europe for a particularly reductionist economistic focus, do we not risk failing to confront the question of Europe *at all*? For such an argument to win support, it would have to be possible to reduce the 'European question' to the issue of the European Union as it currently exists. Can we flout several centuries of history by acting as if it all began with the Maastricht Treaty or the Treaty of Rome? Is that not to embrace the Eurocracy's 'legend of origins'? Over and above the historical dimension, the European question is already posed solely by the fact that, in the course of a few decades, the construction of Europe has created an institutional and political space, which it is all the more futile and dangerous to seek to bypass in that it possesses strategic significance for the struggle against ordo-liberal Europe. No left-wing government in one country can break out of the monetary and normative iron corset on its own. It can create and widen rifts, lead the way – but it will soon require the support of other governments and the backing of social movements in other countries. The point is therefore to construct the conditions for such solidarity now, rather than cultivate the illusion of a return to national sovereignty. If a political crisis must be provoked, it is at the level of Europe as a whole, by breaking

---

30   Ibid., p. 139.
31   Ibid.

with the system of treaties in such a way as to impose a re-foundation of Europe on the basis of European citizenship. At stake is shattering the framework of the EU in order to rescue the project of political Europe.[32]

More broadly, beyond Europe, we must tackle constructing a 'global oppositional arena'. While the immediate terrain of any political struggle is unquestionably the national arena, today even more than yesterday the oligarchic adversary has to operate in a dual political space, national *and* international. This enables the division between national political arenas to be exploited, inciting competition between populations based in separate territories. The task before us is doubtless very different from the construction of the 'Internationals' of the past. But we nevertheless have much to learn from the experience of the International founded in 1864 in St Martin's Hall. First of all because, amid the resurgence of virulent forms of nationalism, it remains true that 'disregard of that bond of brotherhood which ought to exist between the workmen of different countries, and incite them to stand firmly by each other in all their struggles for emancipation, will be chastised by common discomfiture of their incoherent efforts'.[33] Secondly, and perhaps especially, because that International opted for a principle of affiliation that remains entirely justified today: any association or trade union could address its request for affiliation directly

---

32   Systematic recourse to the term 'Europeanism' has the sole function of intellectual intimidation, by disqualifying in advance any separation between Europe and the European Union.

33   'Inaugural Address of the Working Men's International Association', in Karl Marx and Frederick Engels, *Collected Works*, vol. 20, London: Lawrence & Wishart, 1985, p. 12.

to the International, without having to submit its candidature to a national organization purportedly representing the International in a given country.[34] Here we have a way of imparting a practical political significance to internationalism that remains as valuable as ever. We might thus imagine a European and world federation not of different national parties, but of *democratic coalitions* combining political activity at various levels with establishment of the commons, as the concrete bases of an alternative.

Can we already define the programmatic contours of such coalitions? To claim this would be to contravene the very principle of democracy. But that principle involves a minimum of rules, or rather one minimal rule. This basic rule is the rotation of responsibilities, which guarantees the equality of citizens in the exercise of power by enabling each citizen to govern and be governed in turn. Non-re-electability or non-reappointment in public office is the *non-negotiable* rule of any political commons.[35] A remark by Aristotle can help us to better appreciate how respecting it is difficult, but vital, for any democracy worthy of the name. While, in antiquity, all citizens thought it right to 'take their turn of service ... nowadays, for the sake of the advantage which is to be gained from the public revenues and from office, men want to be always in office. One might imagine that the rulers, being sickly, were only kept in health while in office.' And Aristotle adds: 'In that case

---

34   See Mathieu Léonard, *L'émancipation des travailleurs. Une histoire de la Première Internationale*, Paris: La Fabrique, 2011.

35   Pierre Aubenque, *Problèmes aristotéliciens. Philosophie pratique*, Paris: Vrin, 2011, p. 164.

we may be sure that they [will] be hunting after places.'[36] It would be hard to find a more accurate description of the practices whereby the neoliberal oligarchy corrupts any democracy. Conversely, the 'many' (*hoi polloi*) will only prevail over the 'few' (*hoi oligoi*) if they establish this principle and prove capable of ensuring its preservation. Then, and only then, with victory over oligarchy, will Plutus be expelled from the temple of the City.

---

36   Aristotle, *The Politics* and *The Constitution of Athens*, pp. 70–1.

Index